Illustrated and designed by *Robert Riger*

THE
LAST
LOUD
ROAR

Bob Cousy
with
Ed Linn

Series edited by Red Smith

Prentice-Hall, Inc., Englewood Cliffs, New Jersey

The Last Loud Roar
Bob Cousy with Ed Linn
illustrated by Robert Riger

© 1964 by Robert Cousy, Edward Linn and Robert Riger

Library of Congress Catalog Card Number: 64-19989

Printed in the United States of America

T 52401
ISBN: 978-1-5011-4264-2

PRENTICE-HALL INTERNATIONAL, INC., *London*
PRENTICE-HALL OF AUSTRALIA, PTY., LTD., *Sydney*
PRENTICE-HALL OF CANADA, LTD., *Toronto*
PRENTICE-HALL OF INDIA (PRIVATE) LTD., *New Delhi*
PRENTICE-HALL OF JAPAN, INC., *Tokyo*

ENDPAPERS:
Front—Cousy leads Celtics on fast break.
Back—Cousy drives on West off fast break.
Note: "24-second" clock in center of photos.

To my M's,* my comrades and opponents whose inspiration and assistance made all this possible.

FOREWORD

BARON ADOLPH RUPP, the remarkable coach of the University of Kentucky's sometimes remarkable basketball team, was talking about Frank Keaney, the retired coach of Rhode Island State.

"He was a good basketball coach," Adolph said, "and a fine chemistry teacher, and he has the greatest collection of antique spoon-holders in the world. Now, how can they say he's a mean man?"

"Who says he's mean?" a dinner companion asked.

"Everybody!" Adolph said, brandishing his fork.

This was at a coaching clinic in the Catskills, and for a guy who cared little about the game, this threw a new light on basketball. For that matter, the guy knew little about spoon-holders, which went out of style even before napkin rings did, but he agreed with Adolph that any man who felt deeply about spoon-holders could not be all bad.

"Even if he was a roundball coach," the guy thought, "he can't be all bad. But let's face it, would I want my sister to marry a basketball player?"

Some time later, here came George Flynn of Prentice-Hall who used to be a basketball player. He said, "Let's do a series of books on sports." He said, "Let's get the one outstanding man in each game to say whatever he has to say about his game in collaboration with the finest writer in the field, and let's also include the best

11

illustrations that can be had, and we positively will not settle for second-best."

So where would you go for a book on basketball, except to Bob Cousy? For Bob there are more things in heaven and earth than were dreamt of in Naismith's philosophy. For him, basketball has a music of its own, but he also has powerful convictions about people and living, human rights, the rigging of games, and the recruiting of college athletes, officials and coaches, and the individuals he has played against.

He has a great deal to say and when he says it he levels — and may the saints preserve him and the game he dignifies.

Red Smith

AUTHOR'S NOTE

THIS IS the story of a game that has become a way of life for me. I believe it will give the reader an insight and a better understanding why, on one hand to the observer of a sports contest his or her reaction is one of immediate joy or possibly remorse, or just plain entertainment and quickly forgotten as a minute distraction in a passage of time, while for the participant it holds all the answers during the years of activity. The friendship, the camaraderies; the sharing of frustrations, satisfactions, sacrifices; the teamwork; the pride of accomplishment—all the emotions that we all share are here embodied.

Robert Cousy

CONTENTS

PART ONE:

THE TRIP

I IS Tuesday, April 23, a warm day in Worcester, and I wake up early so that I'll be able to see the girls off to school. And that's a change right there.

But that isn't the first thing I think of. The first thought to come to my mind is whether it's my turn to pick up Tommy Heinsohn for the drive into Boston, or whether he is going to pick me up. When you have been riding back and forth together for seven years, the trips tend to blur. But this one is easy. I can remember that it was just as well Tommy had been driving because I had been too tired to keep my eyes open.

"These are the rubber-room days," Tommy says of the last play-off games at the end of the long season. "This is the time of year you just want to get a bunch of rubber bats in a dark rubber room and start whacking away."

A grim ride home it had been. I had gone out on fouls after as lousy a game as I had played in years, and Tommy had been thrown out for two technical fouls, the last one for arguing a call by Richie Powers. With Tommy, "arguing" is a synonym for throwing a small fit.

If we had won that game, as we should have, there'd be no trip to Boston this morning and no flight to Los Angeles this afternoon. We'd have taken the Lakers in five games, the Celtics would be world champions for the sixth time in seven years and I could lie in bed all day today as I had lain in bed all day yesterday.

The fouls bothered me. I had fouled out for the second time in three games, and in the middle game I'd had five fouls called against me. Seventeen fouls in three games; that was more than I'd had in the previous 103 playoff games in my career. And I'm only playing half the time now, at that. Oh boy, either they were calling them closer or I was getting older and slower. It only seems like a few years ago that I was complaining how the old guys would hold and tug and pull at your pants, making up in slyness what they had lost in speed and reflex. But that last foul had been a bad call. It had been worse than that. I had come back in the game in the fourth quarter, after we went cold, to play my only decent ball of the night and we were cutting away at their lead, when with 2 minutes and 58 seconds to play, I dribbled around Frank Selvy in the key and sank a basket that would have closed the gap to 117-115. And when the whistle blew I was sure it was a 3-pointer, because I was sure that Selvy had blocked me. Instead, I found Mendy Rudolph pointing that finger at me and yelling "charge," and not only were the 2 points gone, but I was gone too.

Well, I'd been yelling for years that they should give the defensive man the benefit of the doubt on those block-charge calls, and now that they were doing it I couldn't very well cry. Besides, after thirteen years, I knew how easy it was to blame the officials for your own mistakes.

But, no, looking at it as honestly as possible, it was a bad call. A bad call at a bad time.

And now I have to be honest about something else. For the only time in my life, I'm just as glad we didn't win a game. There, I've said it. For reasons of personal vanity, selfish and unforgivable, I am glad we lost. Not that I'm so reluctant to have the career come to an end. I want it over. I'm so tired I can hardly breathe. Over the past two months, I have developed a nervous tic under my right eye. But I don't want it to end like *that*, with me sitting on the bench after a bad game.

This has been my great fear all year. This is one of the reasons I was ready to retire at the end of the previous season. I have worked thirteen years to build up a name and a reputation. Seventeen years if you count college, nineteen years if you go back to high school, and twenty-one years if you go all the way back to the

20

thirteen-year-old boy picking up a basketball in the playground in St. Albans, New York, and deciding that this was the sport for me.

I smile at that boy now, in the warm, fond way we always smile at the memory of our own youth and our youthful ambitions. And yet it is a different smile, I would suppose, than the average person's because I have had far more success than that boy ever dreamed of; far more success, for that matter, than I ever dreamed of when I got out of college.

There is a conflict in my nature of which I am not entirely unaware. I am a perfectionist, I am proud of my success, and yet I have always been a little bit amazed at the success I have had. Play no soft violins in the background, please, just believe me when I say I have never really believed I was quite as good as the polls and the trophies say I am.

For I have always been afraid that I would not be good enough, even though—if you can follow this—I was cocky enough in my younger days to know that I could handle anything on that court. There was always the fear, before every game, that this would be the night it would all desert me, that this would be the game where everything would go bad and I would be out there, exposed and helpless.

I have tried to analyze this apparent contradiction in my nature through many a night and many a bus ride and many a plane ride, and I know very well that it is this apprehension, this fear of failure, that lifts me up every time I go out onto the court. I know I need it. The trouble is that I know this only intellectually, and only in retrospection. My emotions are unaffected. Before every game, the taste of fear comes back into my mouth and I have to suffer through it all again.

Like right now. Right to the end.

So having smiled at the little boy in St. Albans, I have to smile—a little more wryly—at myself. They're sending men into space, the world is changing all around us, and I'm eating my insides out over a basketball game.

And even this is a contradiction. I know that, relatively, the contribution any athlete or entertainer makes to our society is negligible, that one good teacher is worth the lot of us. I have been known to make parlor speeches about it, to audiences of less-than-enthusiastic teammates. Nothing annoys me more than athletes and entertainers who, having been overpaid and overpraised and overpublicized, come to look upon themselves as having some special merit. And, frankly, I have always been even more annoyed at the people who encourage us to become conceited by looking upon us as a special-privilege class.

Q. *What have you been doing with your life all these years, Mr. Cousy?*

A. *Why, I have been throwing a big ball into a little hoop.*

Q. *And from this, you make a living?*

Still, if honesty is the word for the day, I must admit that I usually end my speech by zeroing in on baseball players. For thirteen years, I've seen the NBA scrambling to stay alive while baseball got all the publicity and the crowds and the glory.

So glory's the key word, is it? That's what it's been all about?

All right—in part it's been for the glory. Yes, I'm jealous of the baseball players. If accomplishment comes 90 percent from self-doubt, then maybe ambition is 90 percent jealousy. Hitting a ball with a bat is no more important to the scheme of things, in other words, than putting a ball in a basket.

So, as I say, I smile to myself as I lie on the bed. I'm thirty-four years old and I'm still a boy having to prove myself over again every time out. But if I've spent my life playing a boy's game, it's still what I do. And because it's what I do I want to be the best. It's not enough to be good enough. It's not enough to be very good. I have to be the best, because that's what it's all about. So while I want to go out on a winning game and a world championship, I also want, most of all, a good last game for myself. For thirteen years, I have thought of the team first and myself second. Here at the end I can indulge myself in this one vanity, without trying to rationalize it or justify it. I've earned the right, I tell myself, to leave as I came. To be remembered for what I was at the top of my game.

Everybody has been telling me how nice it would be to end it in Boston like last year, when the crowd exploded onto the floor as I dribbled out the clock. They almost trampled me to death. But I want it to end in Los Angeles tomorrow night. If we come back to Boston, for a seventh and indisputably final game, the pressure will build stronger than ever as my friends

shower me with affection and attention, and I will enter the game flat again. It's all been too much these past six weeks. I'm just too emotional about these things. Let it end in Los Angeles.

Since we would be returning home immediately after the game, I packed what is called "the full bag," a large suitcase which is partitioned in the middle to make two compartments. On one side go the extra clothes you need for a change, and on the other the game equipment and the soiled clothing. On a road trip, we would take two smaller suitcases, one for our clothes and the other for the equipment since, as you can imagine, your uniform gets so sweaty and smelly after you've played a couple of games that you could separate the clean clothing by a partition, a flap or the Berlin Wall, and they would still end up smelling like a high school locker room.

At somewhere around 10 o'clock, I kiss my wife Missy good-bye and drive over to Heinsohn's house. As Tommy slips into the seat beside me, it suddenly occurs to me, wholly out of context, that I am leaving not only the world of professional basketball, in the sense that it is a sport, but also the world of professional basketball, in the sense that it is a world of giants.

When you constantly move in a world of big men, you become so accustomed to their height that, the human animal being the adaptable mechanism that it is, you automatically discount a few inches from the norm, and look upon a 6'5" man the way you would normally look at a 6-footer. That is, as a man somewhat taller than most people.

Tommy is 6'7", and I find myself looking at him with sudden clarity, the way you do when you are about to leave a house you have been living in for years. Baby, he is big!

"Got a smoke?" I say to him, to kid him, because after years of badgering, I have finally got him to give up smoking. Tommy had been tremendous in both the playoff series, and it is my aim to keep it that way.

Tommy starts to pat the pocket of his jacket before he remembers. "You are a dog of French parentage," he grins.

Tommy is our good-humor man. Like me, he is a graduate of Holy Cross, where he had the gall to break almost all of my scoring records. Unlike me, he is a social animal, a flaming extrovert. I still have a sort of shyness from boyhood and, probably, a faint distrust of strangers. While I'm in my hotel room, sulking, on the road, Tommy will be sitting around the coffee shop, looking for someone to talk to. And if there's anyone still coming around at 4 A.M., Tommy will still be there, talking.

He loves to get up in front of a mike. When we go out together to speak he'll usually be introduced first, and I'll almost always take off my watch and lay it down in front of him, partly to kid him about being such a ham, but also to remind him that if he goes on forever, we'll never get the hell out of there.

I don't want to give the impression that he's just a personality boy. He is intelligent and talented—at Holy Cross he won the Lawler Medal, the annual award given to the athlete having the highest scholastic record. A self-taught cartoonist, he has had some of his caricatures in national magazines. Recently, he has begun to work with oils, and he spends most of his time on the road visiting museums or shopping for art books. With it all, he's a successful insurance salesman. In short, a man of many talents.

But the pleasing personality does not make a better basketball player of him. It probably does the opposite. No fires are burning in Tommy Heinsohn. It has never seemed to me that Tommy loves the game enough to make it hurt. As far as I am concerned, his best season came in his freshman year when he still had to prove what he could do. Not that he doesn't go all out on the floor. Tommy will get so furious at an official's call that he will jump up and down in a tantrum, looking so much like an overgrown six-year-old that afterwards, when we think about it, the rest of us will always give him the needle back in the locker room by such things as inquiring solicitously whether he's hurt his foot.

It's Tommy's off-the-court attitude that has bothered me. Tommy always smoked a little too much, and there's no doubt at all that it affected his wind. His normal gait was to go six or seven minutes at top speed, and then sit down and take a blow.

As we'd drive back and forth between Boston and Worcester through the years, I never stopped telling him that there was no reason why a guy his age shouldn't be able to go at least a full quarter at top speed. And Tommy would always slough me off with a quip or a growl, because he has almost always been our top scorer and he has always been, quite candidly, well satisfied with his performance.

Well, fine. He *should* have been our top scorer because he has all the assets a corner man needs. He's big and he's strong and,

I would say, easily one of the top three or four offensive rebounders in the league. No corner man anywhere has better offensive moves. He's famous most of all for those unorthodox, off-balance, line-drive shots off his ear, which he developed when he first started to play the game, as a kid, in a low-ceilinged gym. If they ever build a court in the leaning tower of Pisa, Tommy will lead the league in scoring.

What makes him so tough is that he has such sure balance and coordination that he can make the plays on the dead run, something most big men can't do, and he has such sure hands that he is an excellent man to feed on the fast break. In these respects, he can make plays that even Pettit or Baylor can't, although obviously they can both do other things that he cannot.

In 1961-62, Tommy had a good enough year, leading our club in scoring again and, in fact, posting the highest average of his career. But scoring is the most misleading statistic in basketball. As far as I was concerned, he had not played up to his standard, and I could tell by his somewhat more subdued attitude that Tommy was not completely happy with his performance either.

This year he got off to a bad start, and by mid-season the Boston sportswriters were writing "What's-the-matter-with-Heinsohn?" columns. They weren't washing him up or anything like that, but it was still not the type of thing to send him into a sound, contented sleep at night.

It was enough, at any rate, to start Tommy muttering that he couldn't understand why they were getting on *his* back all of a sudden, and as soon as I saw he was upset I began to climb on him even more. "You're begining to sound more and more like one of those guys who's always quoting his batting average," I'd tell him. "It isn't a question of what you *are* contributing, as much as what you *can* contribute. The trouble with you is that you don't love the game enough to want to prove to yourself that you can maybe get more out of the basic ability God has given you."

Tommy had something else goading him too. It was taken for granted from the start of the season that the Celtics would meet the Lakers again for the championship, and somewhere along the line Tommy had picked up a complex about Rudy LaRusso, the L.A. forward who guards him. Tommy has come to feel that

LaRusso can do a job on him, possibly because LaRusso very frequently did do a job on him, most particularly in the last two games of last year's playoffs.

LaRusso, who is 6'7" too, has improved tremendously since he came into the league in 1959. Actually, we could have had him as a territorial choice, because he graduated from Dartmouth. His coach, Doggie Julian (my original coach at Holy Cross) recommended him very highly, but he really didn't seem like that good a prospect at the time, and so we took John Richter, who never did make it.

Rudy is a hard-nosed defensive player. I'd heard that not only from Tommy but from other players around the league. And he has studied Tommy's moves very well. Tommy has the habit of bouncing the ball one time before he takes the jump shot, a very bad habit for that good a player, since it means that he has committed himself completely. If he went right up with the jumper at once, he'd have more room, or if he'd give them the head fake, he might get the defensive man to come at him too soon, and give himself a chance to drive by him.

LaRusso doesn't try to block the shot. Except for Russell, who has such a fantastic ability to recover, it is only the weak defensive man who tries to block shots. LaRusso keeps his position, doesn't go for fakes, keeps his weight back and almost forces you to take that outside shot. With Tommy, he'll hold his position, let Tommy come into him with that one bounce, and then he'll dart in and be all over him just as Tommy leaves his feet, not trying to block the shot but just bothering him enough to throw it off.

Tommy knows he's doing it, of course, and we have spent the two weeks before the playoffs hammering away at Tommy to try to eliminate that bounce. But—you do not really do that much thinking on offense. You don't have time to stop and think. *Offense is instinct and defense is concentration*. It's almost as if you are playing two separate games.

Well, when you have to go out there knowing that you're going to have to fight for your life every second of the way, it puts an additional pressure on you. I know, because I used to feel the same way about facing Dugie Martin of the old Minneapolis Lakers. I always had the feeling that Martin was faster and

quicker and more durable than I—probably because he was—and that he was going to stop me cold—possibly because he usually did.

It works the other way too. Syracuse and Cincinnati had come down to the last game of this year fighting for the other playoff berth in our division. I had rooted hard for Cincinnati because if Syracuse won, I'd have to go up against Larry Costello, and next to Martin, Costello is the man who has given me the most trouble through the years. Larry stays on your back, and I know myself well enough to know that if he's going to play a tough defense on me, I'm going to get stubborn about it myself and—against my own self-interest—play a tough defense on him.

Since Larry and I both have the ball about 75 percent of the time, that would give me a fighting chance of going into the L.A. series completely wrung out.

Sam Jones was rooting just as hard for Syracuse, because if we play Cincinnati, all poor Sam has to do is cover Oscar Robertson, who is their playmaker and their scorer and their rebound man and their general all-around wizard and whirling dervish. Oscar is also an inch taller than Sam and he has the ball probably 80 percent of the time. Guarding him is no worse than taking on a windmill with your bare hands.

When we finally got out of the Cincinnati series, after seven games, poor Sam was so happy at getting rid of Oscar that he almost cried. (Oscar averaged 33 points against us in that series, but Sam finally found the way to counterbalance him in that seventh game. Oscar scored 43 points, and Sam, having the best scoring night of his life, had 47.)

So with all these things bugging Tommy, he finally took a grip on himself. Two or three weeks before the playoffs began, he cut out smoking, went into the gym in Worcester and knocked himself out in our own practice sessions. By playoff time he had lost 14 pounds and had really whipped himself into the best shape of his life.

You have to be in good shape against LaRusso, because he will normally score most of his points by muscling in for a second or third effort off the boards. For Heinsohn it becomes a question of letting him come in a step or so and then spinning around and throwing himself into LaRusso, head to head, to try to box him out for the second or two it takes for Russell to pick off the rebound. LaRusso will be pushing just as hard, throwing himself

into Heinsohn, so it's a question of relative strength and, of course, timing. If the ball keeps bouncing around, nothing in the world is going to keep LaRusso out of the action.

Each year, Rudy has been improving. He not only has better moves but he has become far more accurate with his outside shot. While he is not yet a man who can be counted upon for a 20-point game, he can certainly be counted on for between 14 and 18.

Very candidly, I had not expected that we were going to beat Los Angeles in this playoff. Last year's series had gone to overtime of the seventh game, which is about as even as two teams can get. Facing the matter realistically—and pros are, above all, realistic—it seemed to me that they had improved a bit, if only through the acquisition of Dick Barnett, and we had gone back a little, if only because Frank Ramsey was having a bad year.

Well, logic is one thing and the play of the game something else. As it turned out, we could have very easily taken the Lakers in five games, while Cincinnati, which looked pretty soft, had carried us to the seventh game.

The main difference was Tommy Heinsohn. Not only had he led us against Los Angeles, but without him we would have been eliminated by Cincinnati.

The only problem the Celtics have faced in recent years has been the tendency toward complacency. We have been winning for so long, we have such confidence in our ability to take charge when we have to, that we tend to play only as hard as we have to play to win.

Having beaten Cinci pretty much at will for two years, we couldn't bring ourselves to face the fact that they had finally started to jell, even though the figures showed that they had been playing excellent ball since the middle of the year.

There was something else too. Cincinnati got a maximum effort out of every one of their players. We didn't. We had been geared to face Syracuse, and we had great difficulty in suddenly readjusting our thinking. Personally, I had built myself up for that battle with Costello, and when it came up Cincinnati instead, I heaved a sigh of relief and let down. It took at least three games before I could shake myself out of my lethargy.

In the first game, we blew a 22-point lead on our home court,

40

which did tend to make us wonder a bit. Then we went to Cincinnati and blew a 9-point lead in the first half, but came back to win without too much trouble when Heinsohn scored 7 quick points at the start of the second half. It wasn't until the Royals walloped us again, back in Boston, that it finally dawned on us that, boy, we were in a dog fight. The AP lead on that third game ran: "The long reign of the Boston Celtics as NBA champions may be ending."

The one man who was playing great ball for us all along was Heinsohn, because Tommy was still building himself up psychologically for that meeting with LaRusso.

In the key game, the fourth game in Cincinnati, Tommy only scored 19 points, his lowest of the series. But points are meaningless! Tommy played such a great game off both boards that Russell told him back in the locker room that it was the best all-around game he had played in two years.

Back in Boston, Tommy scored 34 points from all over the court to lead us to the victory that finally put us ahead. So naturally we went to Cincinnati, collapsed completely, and had to come back to Boston for the seventh game.

That one was the easiest of all. With Tommy scoring our first 7 points, and 9 of the first 11, we went ahead early and galloped home. Altogether, he averaged 25.9 points, and had a remarkable shooting average of .496.

Off that momentum, he had just been eating LaRusso up. What had made things so rough the previous year was that we had only been able to get an even split in the first two games in Boston. In this year's opener, we were down 13 points in a very sloppy game, but came back to win. The key play came with less than 2 minutes left. Heinsohn, switching men with Sam Jones, found himself covering Jerry West along the right sideline. Jerry threw a fake at him and tried to drive past, but Tommy stayed on top of him, and West had to go up with his jumper. This time, Tommy went up with him beautifully, jamming the ball right back against his hand before he could release it. As the ball bounced over to Sam Jones, Tommy raced down the court, followed by big Gene Wiley (6'10"), and, still in stride, took Sam's pass over his head. But before he shot—and here was the third great move in this one play—Tommy paused just long enough to let the relatively awkward Wiley run into him. That gave Tommy both the basket and the foul, and it gave the Celtics our 3-point margin of victory.

This time we also had a relatively easy time in the second game, winning 113-106, as Tommy outscored LaRusso, 26-12.

Los Angeles took the first game at their own Sports Arena without any trouble, but in the fourth game, which again seemed to be the key, we beat them 108-105. Tommy had 35 points, including the three quick baskets in the last quarter that put us ahead to stay.

After five games, Tommy had a 23.6 average, and LaRusso was down to 13.8.

So here is a man who has come to realize after seven years in the league that he hasn't been getting the most out of his talent. What a waste that is. It isn't enough to be good if you have the ability to be better. It isn't enough to be very good if you have the ability to be great. It certainly isn't enough to simply score a lot of points. I say this over and over again—and I say it, in part, when I talk about Wilt Chamberlain vs. Bill Russell: basketball is a game of intangibles. *The important thing is to play to the peak of your capabilities.*

Not that I'm trying to downgrade Tommy's contribution in past years; he has always been a sort of unsung hero of the team. The Celtics' climb to the top is always pinpointed—quite rightly—with the arrival of Bill Russell halfway through the 1957 season. We had never won a championship until he arrived, and the only time we lost it was when he injured his ankle during the playoffs the following year. What people forget, though, is that Heinsohn had joined the Celtics the same year to give us something else we had always lacked, a big, strong forward who could rebound and score. Everybody also seems to have forgotten that before Russell came back from the Olympic games to join us, Tommy was handling the rebounding along with Jim Loscutoff and doing it well enough so that we were leading the league.

These days, Tommy will sometimes relax almost to the point of laziness on the defensive boards, but that becomes inevitable after you've been playing with Bill Russell for a while. It has happened, to a greater or lesser degree, with every corner man we've ever had. The guy keeps going into the boards, seems to have a good shot at the rebound and then finds Russell's big arm shooting up to snatch it away.

Since the Celtics are geared completely to the fast break, it is only normal for these guys to start to think, "Hey, I'm wasting my time fighting my own man for the ball. While Russ is picking it off, I can release and get a good start down the floor."

And that's just the time, naturally, that the rebound will bounce to the other team, and Tommy's man will be standing alone under the basket. And the fans in the stands will think, "There's that Heinsohn loafing again."

But when Tommy wants to, he can rebound with any forward in the league, including Pettit and Baylor. When he wants to, he can also do an adequate job of all-around defense.

Offense is where he shines, though, and it has been on offense where he has been killing the Lakers dead. Basketball is a game of psychology. As soon as Tommy made the decision to cut out smoking and work himself into the best possible condition he was also beginning to build himself up psychologically toward a showdown meeting with LaRusso.

Our plane does not leave until 3:20 P.M., so Red Auerbach has scheduled a late-morning practice session at the Cambridge YMCA. While the rest of us are taking some light shooting, Heinsohn and Frank Ramsey are off in the corner playing a fairly rugged game of one-on-one to give Rams a chance to work out whatever has been wrong with his game.

The workout over, we all have lunch together, and then Tommy and I climb back into my car for the drive to the airport. We've been booked on a jet flight, with a stopover in Baltimore, and it turns out to be a bumpy, rib-rattling landing. Hey, now, fellows, I've survived thirteen years of these trips. Let's not get careless now.

Throughout the Cinci series, with its relatively short jump, we had traveled on our own chartered plane—a Convair or something —and those charter jobs have built-in compartments that can be converted into card tables. During those plane rides, Buddy La-Roux, our trainer, and I had teamed up against Auerbach and Loscutoff in a nonstop gin game. On the jets we travel "tourist," which I can understand, because it's ridiculous to pay that extra

hundred dollars a man just to sit in the "first-class" section on the other side of the curtain. To keep the gin game going, though, we have to line up, across the aisle from each other, two of us on each side. Instead of jumping back and forth across the aisle to change partners, we have settled down to a permanent pairing: Buddy vs. Auerbach, and me against Lusky.

What makes these partnerships so invigorating is that they give you someone you can keep cursing and second-guessing. "Why didn't you go for the knock?" Arnold screams at Lusky after the first hand. "I give you 30 points and you lose back 35, you rat fink!"

Of course, if you are going to scream at Lusky it is just as well to be the coach, because Lusky is the Mr. Tough Guy of the league.

Jim Loscutoff is 6'5" and he is built no more solid than a bull. (You might as well get used to these figures—the height of a basketball player comes as automatically as the measurements of a beauty queen.) Arnold took him as our surprise first-draft choice eight years ago, which makes him—next to Ramsey and me—the oldest player in point of service on the team. In an age of overwhelming talent, Lusky is a specialist. Perhaps the most narrow specialist in the league. There are, you must remember, only ninety players in the NBA, and all except a very few are signed because they are great shooters. Even those who don't make it usually come in with fabulous reputations. There are, speaking generally, three classes of professionals: the good shooters, the very good shooters, and the great shooters. That leaves very few openings for a mediocre shooter. Lusky is one of them.

He isn't a good ballhandler or dribbler either, and he can't run with us on the fast break. Still, Lusky can do a job for us. And at this point, I can hear the echo coming back, "Yeah, he's your hatchetman." OK, you use your word and I'll use mine. Let's say he's our policeman.

Red Auerbach has always felt more comfortable with a policeman around. Before Lusky came to us, Bob Brannum filled the same role.

Before we get into Lusky's role as a policeman, it should be pointed out that he has some solid assets as a basketball player. He'll get his share of rebounds for you and, for a limited amount

of time, he'll play a tough defense. Satch Sanders has to go against the strong forwards like Baylor and Pettit, and even if he is doing a more than adequate job he will probably pick up his share of fouls. That means that Arnold has got·to rest him. So Lusky comes in and immediately Baylor stops driving. Lusky is the type of guy who just might hurt you if you kept driving in on him, not because he'd deliberately play dirty ball but only because he's not inordinately coordinated. Put that awkwardness along with a tough, aggressive type of play, in which contact is not completely unheard of, and I can assure you that the man he is guarding prefers to hang back and look for the outside shot.

There are a couple of other observations worth making about Loscutoff, the policeman. Rich people don't have to spend their money, and powerful men don't always have to exercise their power in order to inspire respect and fear. It's the same way with Lusky. At this stage of the game, his reputation very frequently does the job for him.

When Lusky comes into a game in Boston, particularly if the game has been getting rough, the home fans let out a happy chant which, loosely translated, means, "Now we're gonna see a little blood flow." This tends to have a very salutary effect on his man, since nobody feels too secure in the other guy's backyard to start with.

On the road, Lusky is usually greeted by a chorus of lusty boos —which has the identical effect of calling the opposing player's attention to the fascinating news that he stands a good chance of being clobbered. I've been hearing for years that basketball is a noncontact game, but never, somehow, from anybody who has seen these poor forwards and centers nursing their wounds in the locker room.

In all honesty, I must say that I am sure I'd hate Loscutoff's guts if we had been playing on opposing teams all these years. We haven't, though. I've been under his protective wing, and I'd be an ingrate not to appreciate it.

There's this about Lusky. He doesn't pick his spots and he doesn't bluff. If things get out of hand, he'll be there with the first punch, an important consideration in a basketball fight where the first punch is frequently the only punch thrown. I've seen him put all 7 feet of big Walt Dukes down for the count, something I never thought I'd ever live to see.

I'll tell you this too. When you're playing in Syracuse—where the home folk come down after you and police protection is, shall we say, sparse and unenthusiastic—it is a comfort to have Lusky around. When one of those riots gets started, you look upon him most fondly.

In all my years with the Celtics, I have never heard Arnold instruct him to go out and rough anybody up. On the other hand, Arnold doesn't go out of his way to admonish Lusky that he would do well to curb his killer instinct and send in an application for the Peace Corps. Far from it. Red will be sitting on the bench, growling, "I'm sick of getting knocked around out there. I'm sick of seeing these guys take advantage of us." And then, whirling quickly, he'll bark, "Get in there, Lusky."

Or Arnold will be moaning, "Look at that guy knocking Heinsohn from pillar to post. . . . Oooooo, did you see what that guy did to Cousy?" And, naturally, "Come on, Lusky, get in there!"

Lusky, being a college man, is quite capable of drawing his own conclusions. Yes, I have always felt that Lusky has a pretty fair idea why he is drawing down a paycheck. While I'm not sure he'd be able to contribute enough offensively to allow any other team the luxury of keeping him on their squad, he has had a place on the Celtics for many years and he has made his contributions to our success.

PART TWO:

THE WAIT

THE PLANE lands in Los Angeles at 9 P.M., right on schedule, and in strict obedience to the voice coming over the loudspeaker system, I turn my watch back three hours to allow for the difference in time. Isn't that great? Three extra hours to sweat out until the start of the game.

For years the Celtics have been staying at Sheraton hotels. This time the Sheraton West is booked up solid. Somebody says that the Milwaukee Braves, who are in town to play the Dodgers, have taken the rooms that would normally have been allotted to us.

At any rate, we are going to stay at the Olympian, a luxury motel on the outskirts of town. The manager is so happy to have us that he is waiting at the airport, in person, to greet us. He even has three or four station wagons standing by to drive us out. And when we arrive there is a banner hanging from the marquee, which reads: WELCOME, RED AUERBACH AND BOSTON CELTICS.

Now isn't that nice. There's nothing like commercial hospitality to give you that warm, choked-up feeling. This guy is *really* making a pitch for our business next season. Well, that isn't fair—I know it isn't fair. The guy has gone out of his way to make things as pleasant as possible. Sure, he'd like our business next year, why shouldn't he?

You're building yourself up to a real foul mood, Cooz, and you're doing it early. Relax, baby. You've got a good 24 hours to brood and scowl and roil up your insides.

For ten years, Bill Sharman and I roomed together on the road, but since Willie left, I've become a loner. I'm sure the other guys think I'm a weirdo, and I'd hate to have to convince a jury of reasonable men that I am not. It's not that I don't enjoy good company. I enjoy the closeness and exchange with the people with whom I have something in common, but otherwise I'm the guy you'll see off in the corner. It's just that I've reached the point where I hate the road. I hate the hotel rooms. I hate the waiting. I don't want to be bugged. I want to be left alone to fight it through by myself. That's why I wanted to retire last year, and that's why the game I am about to play could very well be my last.

The fact of the matter is that I was ready to quit last year and start coaching at Boston College. Everything can add up at once. Two years ago, I had been sounded out about coaching basketball at Holy Cross and I wasn't interested. A year later, when Boston College contacted me, I was ready. Everything can add up so that what was merely difficult and disagreeable becomes intolerable.

It's perfectly obvious to everyone, I think, that you will not submit yourself to indignities at thirty that you would at sixteen. Well, with me it had all come to a head in that one year. Experience doesn't minimize pressure; it magnifies it. With age you become more and more apprehensive about your ability to produce, and you become increasingly protective of the reputation you feel you have established.

The schedule in this league is ridiculous. But the human body can acclimate itself to anything. You sometimes go out and play your best game when you've been hopping around for a full week and have to drag yourself out onto the floor. It's all in the mind; if you think you should be tired, you will be tired. The traveling conditions are nowhere near as difficult as they used to be in the old days, anyway. Everybody flies, and everybody puts their players up in the best hotels.

It wasn't one thing, it was everything. I can remember how exciting it was to make a game trip in my college days, how exciting it was to visit new cities. After you've hit the same cities over and over for thirteen years, the thrill is gone. I had, as I have said, become a hermit, burrowing in my hotel room, barely associating with my teammates and avoiding the close friends I had made through the years.

It had really started years ago, though. Back in 1954, Jack Nichols played for us while he was studying dentistry at Tufts

College, near Boston. He used to have to make special arrangements to fly back right after the game to make his next day's classes, and Frank Ramsey and I latched on to him and began to fly back with him. All I want to do after a game is get the hell out of town, even if I have to catch an all-night coach making half-a-dozen stops.

That's all been building up in me too: all the years of living in hotel rooms while my two daughters were growing up. They were nine and ten years old when I decided to accept the Boston College job, and I knew very well that I had already lost half the years of their lives with me. Your kids grow up, they get married, and they're gone, so all you can really do is enjoy the years of their growth. Nothing you've missed can ever be recaptured; nothing you have failed to do can ever be made up.

They would grow up and be married, and what would I have to remember? Well, I'd have a thousand hotel rooms to remember; I could say I had been all over the world.

Missie had adapted herself to the conditions of my work and had wrapped her life completely around the girls, so I could tell myself that they had each other. And then one day, my older daughter, Marie Colette, said, in what was supposed to be a half-humorous way, "Daddy, why don't you break a leg so you can be home more." And then you know.

And always there is that original point of dignity. When you're young, and the fans shout insults at you, it rolls off your back. You have always been told it's part of the game, and you believe it. Then you start tolling off the years into your thirties, and you begin to ask yourself, "Who says?" It seems to you that you should have more respect for yourself than to submit yourself to it. Never mind all that nonsense about their ticket of admission giving them the right to shout whatever abuse comes to their mind. Who says they have?

I've seen well-dressed, matronly women rush out between halves and try to assault Loscutoff with their handbags. If they did the same thing on the street they'd be arrested. I've seen them jab at him—and the rest of us—with the points of their umbrellas.

In Syracuse and Cincinnati, where you have to pass under the stands on your way to the locker room, they spit down on you. They spit and they throw whatever happens to be in their hands. Why, you never walked to the locker room in Syracuse without automatically ducking your head. Even in St. Louis, which you like to think of as a somewhat more sophisticated city, they spit on you as you're leaving the floor.

In Philadelphia, there used to be a guy who sat right under our basket, in the first row—maybe two feet away from us—and shouted things so obscene that they are not only unprintable but utterly unbelievable. And the poor officials . . . The official would call a foul against the Warriors and have to stand there right in front of this guy while the shot was being taken. The way this guy would crucify him made your stomach turn. Every other time we played there, an official would lose his head so completely that he'd call the cops and order them to throw the guy out. And then owner Eddie Gottlieb would come running down to smooth things over and get the guy a seat in some other part of the arena.

Jack Nichols and I used to talk about him every time we came to town. "If there's ever a riot here," we'd say, "let's just forget everything else and go for him."

And we did get him once. Oh, we got him good. And he never knew it. I told Jack to stand right in front of him as we were warming up, then I went to the foul line, wound up and threw the ball just as hard as I could. Just at the last second, Jack looked the other way and sort of stepped to the side. Well, the ball caught the guy right in the nose; it was one of the best passes I ever threw. His head had been down, and he was stunned. He had no idea what had hit him. He always sat between two buddies, and Jack and I came over, stood right over him and just smiled down happily. And all he could say was, "What happened? . . . what happened?"

Just this year, a guy came running out of the stands after a game in Cincinnati and kicked Red Auerbach right in the shins. Arnold belted him a good left, knocked out a couple of his teeth, and the next thing you know Buddy LaRoux and I were down in the courthouse, at 12:30 on a Sunday night, bailing him out. You get no protection and you can't fight back.

You become cynical about people. They come out for a night's entertainment and they end up a screaming mob. What really upsets you is when you see they have their kids with them. Drunks, you can understand. But how can they bring their children to the game and let them see them acting like animals?

So for the last couple of years, all I could think of was that the time comes in a man's life, dammit, where he shouldn't allow himself to be spat upon for a $2.50 ticket.

It has come to the point where I lie in bed and dread the moment when I have to get up and dress and go to the arena.

And yet, once the game would start, I'd really forget it all. I would always enjoy the exhilaration of the game itself, of the competition. The game itself has been the easiest part all year. With all my worrying, it was impossible for me to have a bad year, because Arnold wouldn't let me. He plays me just enough so that I'm able to hustle all the time I'm in there, and when he sees me tiring, he takes me out. This year, and last year too, he has only been playing me about half a game. Arnold has been pretty much letting me call my own shots.

The only reason I haven't been spending the year coaching college boys, instead of running up and down basketball floors again, is that Walter Brown and Red Auerbach had asked me to play one more year. I felt I owed that to Red, and that I most certainly owed it to Walter. Not that I was making any great sacrifice. I was being paid well for playing, as I have always been well paid.

At any rate, Boston College made arrangements to hold the job open for a year, and everything has worked out to my benefit. I have had a full year to make the kind of orderly transition that athletes seldom get. I have been able to recruit kids for Boston College during the year and sort out my thoughts about coaching; I have been able to organize the public relations work I will be doing; I have been receiving the kind of publicity that is hard to believe, with just about every national magazine that even makes a pass at covering sports doing some kind of a story on me.

The affection has been almost embarrassing. Every city in the league has given me a farewell night, led, of course, by the March 17 affair at the Boston Garden in which I broke down—as I knew I would—and wept and sniffled my way through my speech.

But that was all right. I had been playing before these people for seventeen years; it was like breaking down during a family celebration because you're so happy about having so many nice relatives.

Between you and me, though, I could have done without the nights in the other cities. I fall apart so easily that I rather resent being put on display before people who, whatever their good wishes, are not part of the family. I had a suspicion that the nights were just promotional gimmicks to draw an extra couple of thousand into the house, and while I'm willing to concede that basketball is entitled to use me for that purpose after all I have taken out of the game, I still wasn't too happy about it.

To be called to the center of the floor between halves to wave good-bye to the fans, that's fine. But the speeches and the gifts, I thought, were a bit too much.

But, then, I suppose it all goes back to the cynicism I have developed. It all goes to reinforce my feeling that I've made the right decision in calling it a career before I turn my back on everything and everybody.

For the past three years, I've just stayed in my room, either reading or watching television. Once in a while, if Heinsohn gives me a call, I'll go out and have a beer with him. For the most part, I even have my meals sent up, so I won't have to leave the room at all. I've been doing a lot of reading in hotel rooms these past few years. All of a sudden it has come to me that I could have gotten a whole lot more out of my college education. As I look back on the days at Holy Cross, it seems to me that a lot of the kids were there to put in their four years and pick up a degree before going into business. Next year, I'm coaching basketball at Boston College, and I have to impress upon the kids that they are there primarily to get an education.

I have to laugh at myself, because I know with what cynicism the kids would greet that kind of a speech. Missie is a great crusader. She has an open heart, she holds out a helping hand, she is a collector of stray dogs. And in the end, she always learns that the helping hand gets bruised and stray dogs bite. "You see?" I am forever telling her, "It doesn't pay to be a crusader."

It is of more than passing interest to me that the nickname for the Holy Cross teams is "the Crusaders" and, with all my surface cynicism, I am a fairly bruised crusader myself. Well, at least something took.

Buddy LaRoux signs us all into the motel, but before I go up to the room, I stop at the desk to pick up my key and ask if there are any messages. There are, of course. A tall stack of messages, even more than I expected. Most of them, I know very well, are going to be requests for tickets from friends in the Los Angeles area, for there are a lot of people from back East out on the Coast. There will be requests from friends, from old classmates, from people I have met in my travels, and from friends of friends, some of whose names are completely unrecognizable.

The game has been a sellout for weeks, and there are no tickets, period. Just try to tell that to anybody, though. "Who do you think you're kidding?" you can hear them thinking, "You're Bob Cousy and you can't get tickets?" That's the influence of baseball. A lot of baseball parks seat 50,000 people, and there are always a few tickets to be had even on presumed sellouts. But a basketball arena sits about 15,000 people and when those seats are gone, they are gone. At home, I can at least tell my friends to meet me underneath the Garden, so that I can walk them through the turnstiles. At the very worst, they've got standing room, and with a little luck they might be able to pick up a folding chair somewhere.

In L.A. there is nothing I can do. Normally, the visiting club gets twenty tickets, to be split equally, in theory, among all the players. Actually, Auerbach parcels them out to the players who need them. You get what you can from Arnold, and if you need more you buy them yourself and leave them at the ticket office. You know your friends would rather pay for them themselves than have you pay for them, but it has always seemed easier to buy them than to go through the whole explanation.

As it is, a friend of mine in Worcester had asked me to get six tickets for Joe Scibelli, a guard with the Los Angeles Rams. All through the season, Arnold has been giving me four tickets out of the club's allotment for the playoff games, and I had arranged with Lou Mohs, the Lakers' general manager, to buy two more.

And that closes me out completely as far as tickets are concerned.

The room is a nice one, but I'm not really interested. I'm interested in getting some rest. I run through the messages, which run, predominantly and predictably, to ticket requests. And then I hit one I have to read over twice. An FBI man wants to see me. An FBI man? I know I played a lousy game in Boston, but is that a federal offense? The message on the slip indicates that he wants to ask me about a friend who had given my name as a reference. Just the time for it. Makes my whole day.

I am about to call down to the switchboard to put a DO NOT
DISTURB order on my phone but I very quickly change my mind.
The FBI will bide its time, I suspect, but there is nothing quite
so remorseless as a basketball fan in search of a ticket to a sellout. If the switchboard tells them I can't be disturbed, they'll
know I've checked in, and I'll have a parade marching up to the
door. If the phone rings, I decide, I'll let it.

Oh, oh, the nerve is jumping under my left arm. It will be followed almost immediately, I know, by the tic under my left eye.
There it is. It may last only a few seconds or it may go on for a
couple of minutes. I go to the bathroom and stare into the mir-
ror, knowing very well that I will see nothing except my peering
eyes peering back at me. That's what's been bugging me. I can
feel the tic as clearly as if someone were reaching inside and pulling down . . . *tug* . . . *tug* . . . *tug* . . . and yet there's no outward
sign at all. Am I going off my rocker or something? You're going
nuts, Cooz old boy. You're cracking up, baby. You stayed a year
too long.

I know perfectly well I'm not cracking up, though, because my
doctor back in Worcester has assured me that I am suffering nothing more serious than an attack of nerves brought on by the tension I have been under these past two months. As soon as the
playoffs end, he has assured me, the tic will disappear.

I'm not that worried, because nobody has to tell me at this late
date that I am not the most unemotional man who ever lived. For
most of my life I had nightmares, and the most intriguing part of
them was that I always spoke in French. I had not spoken French
since I was a child, could certainly not carry on a decent conversation awake, and doubted very much whether my nightmares
came equipped with subtitles. After I was married, Missie would
tell me every now and then that I had done a couple of fast laps
around the room during the night, chanting French as I went. The
strange part here was that when she spoke to me in English, I
would answer in English:

Missie: What are you doing, Bob?

Me: I'm running around the room, dear.

It stopped being funny in the summer of 1956, when I went
into residence at my boy's camp in New Hampshire after a particularly rough schedule of personal appearances. The first bad
night came when I leaped out of bed, screaming something or
other in French. When Missie tried to hold me I scooted away

from her, as if I were on a basketball floor, and went racing out of the room, punching open the thick oak door with a sharp right hook and diving clean through the screen door out front.

I had never run into anything during a nightmare before, but this time I ran smack into a big black Buick I had parked in front of the house. Even that didn't wake me, although I could remember afterwards that in my dream I had run into a brick wall while I was trying to escape from a mob.

The only person trying to head me off was, of course, Missie. I broke away from her again, went racing across the grounds and ran flush into a tree. That managed to wake me up. I had a broken finger, my body was covered with small cuts from my glorious leap through the screen door, and both knees were badly swollen from my various collisions with large and immovable objects.

A couple of weeks later, I went through the same routine again, breaking out of the house and racing 200 yards downhill, in my bare feet, over rocks. When I came to this time, I found myself crouching behind a tree in my birthday suit, with my feet all cut and bleeding. I was also holding a club in my hand and waiting patiently to clobber Missie, who was chasing after me.

That scared me, boy. After that, I tied one arm to the bed every night. I don't think it is possible to describe the feeling that comes over you when-you are afraid to lay down your head at night and close your eyes.

When I finally consulted a psychiatrist, as I should have from the beginning, he told me—to my surprise and, I suspect, to my disappointment—that the symptoms were fairly common. "You have what is known as an anxiety complex," he said. "All year, you're on the go, traveling constantly, and then all of a sudden you come to a complete stop. You're on a strict schedule in camp, with no place to go, and your mind has trouble accommodating to the change in routine. Your mental attitude corresponds exactly to the dream. People are holding you back and you are trying to break loose."

It was obvious enough that he wasn't as concerned as I was. "Don't worry about it," he said. "People seldom hurt themselves in this kind of thing."

I'm sitting there, so bruised I can hardly walk, and he's telling me people don't hurt themselves. I also would have been somewhat more reassured if I hadn't been aware that if I had

59

broken through the screen door in back, instead of the one in front, I would have gone tumbling down a 40-foot drop into a lake.

The psychiatrist prescribed tranquilizers, to be taken before I went to bed, and the nightmares stopped.

So the nightmares had come as the result of a relaxation of tension, and the tic is the result of the tension itself. They've got me coming and going.

I run a hot bath and soak for a while to relax myself—not only emotionally but physically. Here's another habit I've developed of late, another sign of encroaching age. Soak your weary bones, Cooz. *Aaaaaaah.*

The phone is ringing and the nerve is jumping. Let it ring, Cooz, let it jump.

As I lie there in the hot tub, I close my eyes and see myself on the court guarding Frank Selvy. I am picking him up in the backcourt and I very quickly throw a fake at him to make him get rid of the ball—because the less he has the ball the easier my job becomes.

Selvy passes off to a blue uniform, and now I'm guarding him without the ball, my left foot forward, between him and the ball-carrier, to close off the easy pass return. This is one of the tricks I have picked up over the last couple of years to try to preserve as much energy as possible. I have first made him get rid of the ball and now, simply by putting my inside foot forward, I'm making the other guy think twice before he passes it back. If Selvy wants the ball he has to go get it, which means he not only has to swing around me, but he has to crisscross his own man, something coaches instruct their players to avoid whenever possible.

My theory is simple enough. Selvy is the man who is supposed to bring the ball up court for the Lakers, which means he'll be handling the ball 75 percent of the time he's in the game. It is possible that by playing him this way, he'll be handling the ball only 60 percent of the time, and that means that percentagewise .he'll only be taking about a dozen shots instead of 20 or 25.

That's the theory I've been using, anyway. The only trouble with it is that when you get up against a strong kid he'll just overpower you no matter what you do, on youth and height and sheer animal spirit.

With Selvy, it really doesn't work that way, anyway. Selvy is the "other guard" in the Laker offense. He is the guard who

doesn't score. Selvy's job is to get the ball to Baylor and West. That makes my job relatively easy, because he's not looking to shoot, himself; he's not looking to get me one-on-one so he can create his own opportunities.

Selvy is only going to shoot if I give him so much room that I'm challenging him to shoot, insulting him to the point where he has to shoot. I have not the slightest intention of doing that to Frank, because he is an excellent shooter. Give him room and he'll hit that jumper nine times out of ten. I can remember a couple of times early in the season when I gave him the first couple of shots and he went on to develop a hot hand and score somewhere up in the 30's. Frank is like all the rest of us. If he gets three or four hoops early, he's going to forget about throwing the ball to Baylor or anybody else. He's going to bomb that thing himself. Schaus might ask him what the hell he's doing if he's shooting and missing, but nobody bawls out a man who's hitting.

But since, as I say, he normally isn't looking to create his own scoring opportunities, he's a relatively easy man to guard. He doesn't have a stationary shot, he takes a jump shot from the outside. But—again because of his function on the team—he won't

shoot the jumper unless I give him room. So I stay on him. If I have played off him and have to charge toward him when he gets the ball he's going to drive on me, and he's a fairly good driver. He has enough speed and a good enough fake to get by me every time.

So the overall strategy against him, for four separate reasons, is to stay as close as possible to him when he hasn't got the ball. First, to make him get rid of it, then to make it difficult for him to get it back and, once he has it, to discourage him from taking his shot, and lastly, to prevent him from driving on me.

That's simple enough. Lying there in the tub, I try to review his moves more minutely. We are all stereotyped to *some* degree; we do what we do. The trick is to know what he's going to do *when* he does it and, knowing it, to stop him. That's the real trick. Oscar Robertson could call out all his moves to me, and I still wouldn't come close to stopping him.

Not only doesn't Selvy have a set shot, he will very seldom take the jump shot from a stationary position. He likes to take a bounce and then kind of jump into you as he's shooting, getting his power from his body momentum and, possibly, luring you into a foul.

I also know that if he decides to drive, he will usually fake slowly to the left and then swing to the right, not with the usual quick, jerky motion but in deceptively long, loping strides.

I go over these moves of his in my head, me against Selvy, as if I'm running a game film over and over. I run over every move he makes, and every move I am going to make to counteract them. Me against Selvy.

And, of course, he never makes a wrong move, he does nothing wrong. In thirteen years, my man has never done anything wrong while I was previewing a game in my head, and I have done darn few things right. I am doing something else in addition to cataloging Frank Selvy. I am working myself into a rage. I'm working up a hatred against him. A competitive hatred. I don't know how it works with anybody else, but once I've locked myself in a room and concentrated on my opponent—me against him—hour after hour, my emotions will be so taut by the time I take the court that if you plucked on me I'd twang.

I will have built myself up to such a pitch that when all that emotion begins to discharge itself at the opening tap, it will generate a flow of energy that will carry me through the whole game.

One of my troubles has been that it has become increasingly difficult to generate any kind of enthusiasm, let alone emotion, before a game. It is simply impossible to work yourself up to that kind of pitch 112 times a season. I'm not a machine. I can't press a button and turn it on and off at will.

For this one, I don't have to worry. For this one, you could put a chorus line of dancing girls in front of me, and all I'd see would be Frank Selvy, faking slowly to the left and then, quickly, in those long, loping strides. . . .

Me against Selvy.

The other man I might possibly be guarding during the evening is Dick Barnett, who comes in for both Selvy and West and really amounts, in effect, to a third starting guard. No two men could possibly be more different than Selvy and Barnett. Barnett is an individualist and, even worse, a 6'4" individualist. Every time he gets his hands on the ball Barnett is going to shoot.

This is Barnett's first year with Los Angeles, and he has helped them tremendously. It's a funny thing about reserve players, particularly if they are specialists. They are like pegs in a board. A square peg isn't much use when you have a round hole, but if you move it over to a board that is in desperate need of a square peg, it becomes another story.

Barnett was discovered by Paul Seymour, the Syracuse coach. He came into the league with a tremendous buildup, and he was, to give him his due, very clever with the ball and a fantastic shooter. Barnett is probably as good a shooter as there is in the league, which is saying a great deal. But Syracuse, more than any other team in the league, has always had to play a precise, patterned brand of ball. They have never had a really good big man. They have to run and they have to pass and, because they don't control the boards, their margin for error was always very slight. In order to win, they have to get a maximum contribution from every player, which means that every player has to get his chance at his best shots.

Barnett scored very well whenever he was in the game, but because his style is to get the ball and go into business for himself he didn't fit in with them at all. Seymour had to get rid of him after a year and a half, and Barnett spent a year in the newly formed American Basketball League.

This year, he signed with Los Angeles, a team that could put his abilities to use.

In past years, Los Angeles had been dependent almost entirely upon Elgin Baylor and Jerry West. Giving them the 70 points they figured to score between them on an average night, the Lakers still needed another 50 points or so to win. All right, La-Russo had come to the point where he'll get his 15 to 17, but they still had to find 35 more points somewhere.

By adding Barnett, they now had another 15-17 points, and that meant they only have to get 18-20 points from the rest of the team. But he is also valuable from the purely psychological viewpoint. One of the reasons for the Celtics' great success over the years, given our strong starting team, was that we had such a strong bench that we were always able to keep the pressure on the other team offensively. If one of us were having a bad night, someone else would always seem to come off the bench and make up for it. When Sharman or I would take a rest, Sam Jones and K. C. Jones would come out and run the other team right off their feet. During this past season, we didn't even have a player averaging 20 points. Everybody contributes.

On a professional level, this is absolutely vital. The team that wins the championship has to be able to keep the pressure on the other guys for 48 solid minutes.

In past years, when West went out, you used to be able to heave a sigh of relief and, feeling fairly secure with half the scoring punch out of the game, you would pick up the pace and put on the pressure yourself to try to break it open. But Barnett, whatever his weaknesses, will frequently give you just as strong a point-per-minute production as Jerry. And even more than that, he is a guy who can come up with a hot hand and hit five or six baskets in a row because he has that great touch and he can hit his jump shot from any place on the floor. And while he's not fast, he has very deceptive moves and a good change of pace.

Instead of getting those ten minutes of relief, you now found yourself under assault, with nothing to look forward to but the return of a nicely rested Jerry West, ready to bomb you some more himself.

And because he was getting in the game more and contributing to his team's effort, Barnett had been hustling on defense more than he ever had at Syracuse.

Barnett, in fact, had beat us the first two times we faced each other this season, to help the Lakers off to their zooming start. The first game was in Boston, where he scored 36 points, and the second in Los Angeles, when he scored 38.

We were playing Los Angeles again two nights later, and so after he had beaten us that second game, I asked Arnold to let me cover him. For despite everything I have said about his ability as a shooter, I just didn't see him as a man who should be getting that kind of production.

He has weaknesses. In the first place, he doesn't move without the ball, and once he gets it he's looking to do nothing except shoot.

But more than anything else, Barnett is a left-hander, and *he is left all the way*. It's a strange thing about left-handed basketball players. You'd think that living in a right-hander's world, they'd become almost ambidextrous. For some reason, it seems to work the other way. Although almost all right-handers can make a fair stab at putting the ball up with their left hand or dribbing to their left, it's very seldom you find a lefty who isn't almost helpless with his right hand.

Nobody is more ineffective that way than Barnett. To me that meant he could be defensed.

I locked myself in that hotel for the full day and a half and went into one of my trances. By the time I got out onto the floor I had worked myself into such a rage that, I swear, if Barnett had as much as said hello to me, I'd have burst into tears.

I stayed right on his jock, guarding him without the ball, not to make my own defensive job easier this time—in this instance, I had set myself to play a hard-nosed defensive game, expending every bit of energy I had—but because the only way you can stop a good scorer is to keep the ball out of his hands. When you get a man like Barnett, who doesn't move without the ball, you have a good fighting chance to keep that ball away from him.

Mostly, though, I wanted to prove to myself that he could be pretty well stopped if he were overplayed completely to his left side. Normally, you play your man head to head, with your body squared against his. If you have a man who tends to go to his left side most of the time, you play him half-a-man to the left; that is, with your shoulder bissecting his midsection. You're letting him see the lane on his right-hand side and more or less challenging him to take it. With Barnett, I played him not just half-a-man but a full man to his left, offering him the whole right-hand lane any time he wanted it.

If he still insisted on going to his left, he now had to take a complete semicircular route around me, which would take him out almost to the baseline. While he was describing that circle, I had only to slice straight across the diameter and cut him off.

His best bet would seem to be to take the open lane, because if he can get a quick step on me—and he has the moves to get it— he can drive around me with a right-hand dribble and still have time to shift the ball to his left-hand when he shoots. He's also going to hit a certain amount of jump shots, no matter how tightly I play him, partly because he's so deadly with it and partly because he's got 3 inches on me. The best defensive player in the world can't stop a good shooter, anyway. All he can do is a better job than the next guy.

What I am doing, then, is playing percentage. Because that's what pro ball comes down to, percentage to the *nth* degree.

I guarded him with and without the ball for the whole first half and held him to about 8 points, but I left the floor knowing I had been in a game. When K. C. Jones took over for the third quarter I instructed him to do the same thing, because once you've worked yourself up to this kind of effort you get to the point where all you can think of is that you want to shut the son of a gun out.

For me to instruct K. C. on defense proves how worked up I was, because Case is a really hard-nosed defensive player, as good a defensive man as you'll find in any backcourt anywhere. We didn't stop Barnett cold by any means. But we did hold him to a respectable figure, and we did win the game.

Again, we're back to psychology. When you take a man who is hungry for the ball and cover him that closely, you are frustrating him. You are making him press. If he misses his first couple of shots, he may stop shooting altogether, and then you've taken all his value from him.

This is what I tell my kids at camp. When you go out to guard a man, you should be able to tell after 2 or 3 minutes whether he is left-handed or right-handed, whether he shoots from the outside at all, and—assuming he does—whether he can hit from out there. Whether he drives, and—if he does—whether he prefers to drive to his right or his left. You should also have a pretty good line on his fakes.

Once you are consciously looking for those things, you are also looking for the best way to stop him from doing what he wants to do. And that means you are playing defense, not just chasing your man up and down the floor.

It cuts both ways. You can tell when the guy covering you is all hopped up too. I know very well that I am a powerful psychological stimulant to all my opponents. Boy, the way they come running out there you can practically hear the pep talk their coach has just given them. That damn saliva is flowing out of the corners of their mouths, and their fangs are bared as if they're ready to eat me up alive.

I'm sure I have always scored the majority of my points in the second half, because I've never thought it worthwhile to expend the energy that would be needed to fight them off while they were still in the grip of that first blood-lust. I'd just go along for the first half, talking the shots that came to me but not really pushing for any others, not really looking to make my own opportunities.

You have to be a basketball player to appreciate what fantastic concentration and willpower is needed to sustain that kind of blanketing defense for 48 minutes while also performing your offensive job. The only man who could do it was that little bugger, Dugie Martin, although I must add that Larry Costello comes awfully close.

By the second half, I'd begin to look for signs of a physical and psychological weakening. They're easy enough to spot. During the first part of the game, Russell would give me a pick, and the guy would throw an elbow over Russ's shoulder and try to fight his way over the top. This is the correct way to neutralize the pick. It is also the tough and bruising way. He'll fight his way over during the first quarter, and he'll fight his way through in the second quarter. As the third quarter wears on, I will suddenly become aware that he is begining to slide between Russ and the defensive man who is guarding Russ. The saliva isn't flowing quite as freely anymore, and he is quite willing to give me my outside shot. By the fourth quarter, he may have lost his concentration so completely that he is going *behind* the other defensive man, which means there are now two men between me and the guy who is supposed to be guarding me.

In a situation like that, I can develop almost any kind of play I want to. He doesn't *know* he's doing it, mind you. If he knew it, he wouldn't be doing it. He is just too physically and mentally spent to concentrate on what is going on.

This is my opportunity to let out a couple of notches and begin to really look for my own shots, because if I can hit three or four quick baskets, my man will suddenly realize that all the work and sweat of the first half has gone for nothing. If there's anything more discouraging than to see half an hour's work disappear in a couple of minutes I don't know what it is. Once he gets that sinking feeling in his stomach, it's up to me to pull out the throttle and try to break things wide open.

It's hard to go wrong when you've got human nature working for you.

I've never had any reputation as a defensive player myself, except as a poor one, although, frankly, I think I was always a better defensive player than most people thought. I had quick hands and quick reflexes and, when it was necessary, I could concentrate well enough to do the job. I was always aware, however, that I was supposed to conserve my energy for the offense. While Arnold never told me that in so many words, I couldn't help but note that he was always very careful to assign the top scorer in the other team's backcourt to Bill Sharman and, more recently, to Sam Jones.

Sharman is a good example of a man who made himself into a top defensive player through sheer concentration, hard work and native stubbornness. Willie had fantastic concentration and ferocious pride. In the early days, Bill had some kind of feud going with Andy Phillip, who was then at Ft. Wayne. Bill would latch himself onto Andy from the opening tap and never let him get more than a couple of feet away.

The rest of us would fall back behind halfcourt to set up a normal defense, but Bill would pick Andy up right at the out-of-bounds line and follow him shoulder to shoulder. He was so determined to shut him out that you could almost never get him to switch to another man, even when a switch was clearly called for.

And, boy, if he ever did switch, and Phillip scored on the other man, Willie would climb all over the poor guy and cuss him out something awful.

What made the whole thing so ridiculous was that Andy was an easy man to defend against. Andy was a real playmaker and he never looked for his own shots. If Bill had just done an adequate job, there is no reason to think that Andy would have scored appreciably more than he did. For reasons known only to himself, though, it was important to Willie that he stop Phillip cold, and he was willing to pay the price. There are things you do for the team and there are things you do for yourself.

Willie remained a hell of a defensive man right to the end. In his last year, 1961, we played Syracuse in the semifinals. The Nats were getting most of their scoring out of their backcourtmen, Costello and Greer, and in talking the series over ahead of time, Willie and I decided to keep the pressure on them, to play them without the ball every minute of the way, even if it meant—as it obviously did—that we had to take a little away from our offense. Costello, who is tough enough under any circumstances, got sore enough when he saw what I was doing to press me even further, and we pretty well canceled each other out.

Greer had been playing brilliantly up to that point, but Willie not only held him to 47 points in five games—27 in the last four games—he held him to an average of nine shots in the last four games. That's almost like pitching a shutout. While he was doing it, Willie also had a great series offensively and we breezed past them, four games to one.

But Sharman has been gone a couple of years now, and I am lying in the tub, seeing Barnett take that lane on the right and drive in, shifting hands nicely and scoring. I rerun it again in my head, trying to keep him from getting that first big step on me, but this time he fakes nicely to his left, slaps the ball behind his back, picks it up with his right hand again and dribbles right by me. To hell with you, Barnett, I'll probably never even get to cover you. I'll leave you to K. C. Jones and get back to watching myself being fooled by Selvy.

I lift myself out of the tub and put on my pajamas. I'm about to call down to room service to order dinner when I realize that the phone is ringing—that in fact it has been ringing steadily.

The novel I have with me is Allen Drury's *Shade of Difference*. I lie down and try to read it, but unfortunately it doesn't read as quickly as his first one, and I find my mind racing onto the game tomorrow night. I've turned three or four pages before I realize that although my eyes have been following the words, I haven't digested a thing. So I go back and try again, turn the page again and realize again that I still haven't understood a word of it— possibly because I have been trying to move the Laker defense on a 3-on-2 break.

Giving up on Drury, I turn on the television set and stare at it intently for almost 15 minutes. It is not until the commercial comes on that I realize I haven't seen a darn thing.

I know what I'll do. I am to be the guest of honor in an affair we are holding in Worcester to raise money for the Cystic Fibrosis Fund, for which I am the honorary Massachusetts chairman. This is as good a time as any to write my speech.

Just as I'm starting, there is a knock on the door. Standing outside is a huge bearded man, accompanied by a huge Great Dane.

He is not a representative of the local chapter of Beatniks of America, though, he is a friend of mine, Ed Leiser. I've known Ed since I worked up at Tamarack Lodge in the Catskills during my high school days.

One of the pleasant things about the franchise transfers to Los Angeles and San Francisco was that you not only left the cold and snow behind for a few days, but that you ran into a lot of people you hadn't seen in years. Ed Leiser was one of them. The first time I'd bumped into Ed came when Bill Sharman and I went to a nightclub to see Roberta Sherwood. After the show, Willie and I walked out to the lobby and found Walter Winchell—who had introduced Miss Sherwood—holding court. It was just at the time of the Lana Turner stabbing case, and Winchell was letting it be known to his assembled admirers that none of those hoods had ever frightened him. "Those guys are always sending me threatening letters too," he said, "but I don't worry as long as I've got the old pacifier here."

And darned if he didn't. Sharman always used to say that people recognized me at the darndest time, and Willie had a point.

Just as Winchell went down into his pocket and was coming out with the old pacifier, a big guy standing alongside him spun around and yelled, "Bob Cousy!"

Well, Winchell spun around too, gun and all, and my boy Sharman liked to jump under the table.

The big guy, of course, was Leiser, who was working for Winchell as a sort of combination bodyguard and press agent. Whenever we came to the Coast after that, I'd usually see him and, more often than not, get him some tickets. I assumed he had come up now to ask if I could get him any for tomorrow's game.

Fortunately, I knew him well enough to be able to tell him that I was busy writing a speech and that I was in one of those moods where I wanted to be alone.

I finish the speech at about 11 P.M., and call down to put a DO NOT DISTURB on my phone. And now at last I go to bed, playing the game over in my mind and counting the tics in my eye until I doze off.

When I wake up, I decide to go out into the civilized world and have breakfast. Auerbach is there, sitting in the motel restaurant with Saul Mariaschin, the old Harvard basketball star who played briefly with the Celtics just before I arrived on the scene. Saul is now living in California. I still have no appetite, so I limit my order to juice, coffee and an English muffin. Tommy Heinsohn joins us, and then a couple of guys come over and identify themselves as the FBI agents who had left the message for me.

Since they are going to ask me about someone whom I presumably know, I suggest we go over to their table. It turns out that they want information about a former basketball player who has applied to get into the bureau. As so frequently happens, it is a guy I have never heard of in my life. "You'd be surprised," I tell them, "how often people come up with regards from a very good friend of mine and, you know, it's a guy I've never heard of."

When that first started to happen I used to go blank and tell them, with my native honesty, that the name was unfamiliar. With a little maturity, I have come to realize that if name-dropping is a sin, it is one we are all guilty of, myself included. You meet somebody once at an affair, and he takes a personal interest in you, follows you in the papers, and the time eventually comes when he believes there is a relationship between you that doesn't in fact exist. Instead of making the guy look ridiculous to his friend, I shake the friend's hand and say, "Yeah, how is good old Joe? Tell him I said hello."

As we talk, it develops that the FBI agents are basketball fans themselves. One of them has played a bit of ball back East. So we sit there for about 10 minutes talking basketball.

When I return to the original table, Heinsohn tells me that he is going to spend the afternoon going through an electronics plant. He's looking for company—namely, me.

"Of all the things you could have found for me to do today," I tell him, "touring an electronics plant ranks right at the bottom of the list. Are you crazy or something?"

On the way back to my room, I pass the press room, see some of the Boston writers sitting there with Lusky, and decide to go in and shoot the bull for a while. These are my guys: Jack Barry and Clif Keane of the *Globe*; Bill McSweeney and Murray Kramer of the *Record-American*; Fred Foye and Hugh Wheelwright of the *American*; Joe Looney, the *Herald*; Phil Elderken, the *Christian Science Monitor*; Howie Iverson, the Lowell *Sun*; and Lin Raymond of the Quincy *Patriot-Ledger*.

I've known many of them since my freshman days at Holy Cross, and in all those years we have never had a harsh word. There's never even been a story that I could complain about, excessive praise being very hard to find fault with.

Bob Wolff, who was going to be telecasting the game nationally, had told me he might be able to get in a plug for Cystic, so when I return to my own room I sit down at the table to write down a few facts for him. I'm beginning to get edgy now. I want this damn game so bad I can taste it. That isn't all I can taste either. I am beginning to make frequent trips to the bathroom. That's another thing about the rising nervousness before this kind of game; I find myself going to the bathroom continually—and I mean continually.

I have to laugh. I was on the Mike Wallace show at the time he was in full flower, and you remember how he was. If you said, "It's a nice day, isn't it, Mike?" he'd jump in and bark, "It is, is it? Just what did you mean by that?" When he asked me what it was like before a big game, I tried to tell him how the pressure kept building up until it became almost unbearable. "But what are the manifestations of this pressure?" he kept saying. "Exactly how do you feel?"

Nothing I could say seemed to satisfy him, so finally I blurted, "Well, I go to the toilet much more often."

Wow! The show was on tape. It was syndicated all over the country, and for months I kept getting letters protesting my unspeakable vulgarity. But whether one speaks of one's bladder weaknesses in public or not, that's how it is. During the season, it never bothers you but, boy, you get into one of those playoff games, and you're running to the head like you've got a hole in the tank.

There is a little balcony outside my window, overlooking an indoor pool. I'm so edgy by now that I move the table out there. Bill McSweeney, Clif Keane and Murray Kramer are seated just below me, playing hearts, and Jack Barry, who doesn't play, is kibitzing. While writing, I pick up the conversation from the press room. As usual, Clif Keane has the needle out for me, and I, obligingly, needle him right back. Clif is always on me, and I know he'd be disappointed if I didn't give it back to him.

I finish writing a little background information for Bob Wolff, hoping devoutly that he can use it. I'm thankful for the chance to get my mind on something else, and I'm even more thankful for the opportunity to get some national publicity for Cystic.

Here is one way an athlete can be of some help to society, by using his name and his reputation and his good will to aid a good cause. From time to time, I had been asked to associate myself with various charities, and while all of them are worthy, I had always felt that if I were going to involve myself in that kind of thing, I wanted to find an organization that really needed my help. It's like basketball or anything else. If you work hard, you want to be able to see the results.

In 1956, a friend of mine in the radio business, whose only boy had died of cystic fibrosis, asked me if I would become honorary chairman of their annual fund drive. It seemed to me that, aside from the friendship that was involved, this might be exactly what I had been waiting for. I have been honorary chairman of the Massachusetts drive ever since.

Cystic fibrosis is a fatal disease that afflicts children. Few people can tell you what it is, even now, which is probably not too surprising since it was not even diagnosed as a separate disease until 1933. The year before I took over, the total proceeds raised in the state came to about $4,000. This past year, we raised a little over $90,000.

Cystic fibrosis is a disease which affects the child's pancreas. The pancreatic juices stop flowing normally, and the kids cannot digest their food. As a result, they develop ravenous appetites and, at the same time, they become emaciated to the point where their stomachs protrude. As a side effect, a mucous substance fills their lungs, bringing on a hacking cough. It is this congestion in the lungs that usually kills them, even before they can die of malnutrition.

When we first started, death was only a matter of months. We have progressed to the point where the doctors have been able to keep a child alive until the age of twenty, and the child can lead a normal life

I've visited the victims in so many hospitals, and it just tears your heart out. They sit up in bed and they talk to you and laugh with you, and except for looking so thin, they seem perfectly normal. You are having a long chat with some marvelous little six-year-old girl, cute as a button and just as alert and vivacious as she can possibly be, and suddenly she is telling you, "Yes, I'm feeling fine. I'm going home tomorrow."

And your heart stops beating. Because she is telling you, although she does not know it, that she will be dead before the week is over.

What kills you is that you know it would take, relatively speaking, such a small amount of money to find the cure. We have doctors who are devoting all their energies to it now, and they assure us that it is only a matter of time and money. It is the money, of course, which can buy up the time.

So exposure is very important to us. There is no way people can help us unless they know what is involved, and there is no reason for them to want to help unless they know how much their help is needed.

I have always liked to eat about 4 hours before a game. At 3 P.M., after a long afternoon of increasing tension, I go down to the restaurant. A few of the other players are there too, but I prefer to sit at a table by myself. In the old days, I was a faithful follower of the athlete's dictum of strength through steak. In recent years, I have broken out of that routine. California has the best beef stew in the country, but my stomach is tied into such knots and the tension has gripped me so completely that I do little more than pick at it.

At last I give up, go back to the room and lie down, hoping to catch a quick nap. No chance. There is no attempt to read any more. The television set is ignored. If my life depended upon it, I could not think of anything except Frank Selvy and the game. If you asked me the names of my daughters—quick—I'd be hard put to tell you. The thousands of games I have played mean nothing. Whatever success I have had in the past is forgotten. It all seems like a mistake. I can see Elgin Baylor, with that remarkable body control of his, that incredible strength and unbelievable coordination, running wild on the court. Elgin scored 61 points against us in one of last year's playoff games, and I know very well that he can score 61 or better on any given night.

No, it isn't tension that has tied up my stomach, it is fear. I am, in short, in exactly the frame of mind I should be. At the moment, as I have said, I don't know it. I'm too scared to know it.

At 6 o'clock we are to meet in the lobby. In these playoff games, Arnold insists that all the players leave the hotel together.

For some reason, I have a hard time pulling myself out of the bed. I'm beginning to feel weak and, anyway, I don't want to have to wait around in the lobby. It's almost 6 before I finally drag myself up and begin to repack my suitcase. By the time I go down to the lobby, only Tommy Heinsohn is still there, waiting for me. The management is once again supplying the cars to take us to the Sports Arena. One of the cars has already left, and the other is just pulling away. "Come on," Tommy says, impatiently, "You're with me. Jeez, everybody else has gone."

The car, for some reason or other, isn't out in front. It is waiting at the ramp of the garage, and the garage is a good distance behind the motel.

When we arrive at the Arena, I still have one task to perform, the matter of the tickets for Scibelli. Instead of going right to the locker room with Tommy, I walk through the underpinnings of the Arena to the front office to buy my two tickets from Lou Mohs. Lou is a heavy-set, gray-haired, soft-spoken man. A nice guy. I add Scibelli's two tickets to the four I already have, and Lou puts them in an envelope and hands it to the office boy to bring out to the ticket window.

PART THREE:

PRE-GAME

THE Sports Arena locker room is so set up that it is, in effect, two locker rooms running parallel to each other. The trainer's room is in between them. There is, of course, plenty of room in the front locker room to accommodate the ten men on a basketball team and it is customary for the players to dress together. But I'm something of a hermit. With this obsession of mine to be alone, I have formed the habit of dressing in the back locker room whenever we play in L.A.

For one thing, Los Angeles is a town where we can count on having a lot of visitors dropping by to say hello. Red has a lot of friends among show-business people, and show-business people are in the habit of dropping around backstage. Red likes to have someone around to laugh with, that's his system for holding off the tension. Naturally enough, he brings them around and introduces them to the players. They mean well enough, but there isn't a lot they can say, except to ask you how you're feeling. If I had a dollar for every time I've been asked how I felt I'd be rich enough to give Rockefeller a run for public office. Sometimes it seems that the main preoccupation of the world is how I feel. Well, I'm feeling lousy, sweetie, that's how I feel. I don't want to see anybody, I don't want to shake hands with anybody, I don't want to go through the amenities, and I don't want to tell people that I'm feeling fine, thanks.

Show-business types are always on, anyway, and I don't feel in any great need of songs, dances or funny stories at the moment.

This time I find Frank Ramsey in the back locker room undressing slowly. It has been a brutal year for Rams, and he has formed the habit of getting away from everything and everybody too. Rams, in fact, could give me brooding lessons.

Rams is sitting on a stool, in front of a locker at the far corner of the room. As soon as he gets into uniform, the locker boy comes in with a hot towel for him to apply to his knee. Normally, during the season, I try to arrive less than an hour before the start of the game so that I can cut the wait down to a minimum. Rams will arrive two hours or more before the game, before anyone else is there, and just sit there in the corner all by himself.

The Sports Arena dressing rooms are not only split into two sections, but each of them has a split personality. On the far side of the room is a long row of lockers. The other side looks like the dressing room of a theater. The wall is covered by a row of mirrors, each with a little light above it and a shelf below.

It takes me no more than 5 minutes to get into uniform, which means I now have nothing to do for the next hour and a half except wait for the game to start. This is the time that really bugs me. I'm trapped. There's no place to go except to the head, and I shall be making that trip often. Ramsey will be making the trip often too.

There is a long bench running in front of the mirrored wall. I fold up my jacket to make a pillow for myself and lie down. I close my eyes and I see Frank Selvy.

After a long spell of silence, I speak. The words are well worth waiting for. "Jeez, Rams," I say, "we got to get this one."

"We can't let it go to the seventh," he says.

"That's right. Anything can happen in that seventh."

"Those bastards are going to be tough tonight. They were tough enough in Boston."

We're like two kids in a cemetery, scaring each other. Each of us is trying to rev the other guy up and each of us is trying to pretend he is not trying to rev himself up a little too. You have to say something, you know, to let some of the steam escape, and while it is wholly unnecessary on either count, because we are both ready to explode, we will repeat the same pat, hackneyed phrases over and over for the next hour and a half.

"That Baylor," he says, grimly. "What an animal he is. But Satch and Russ have been doing a job on him. They've been doing a job."

"That West," I say. "I tell you one thing, Rams. We better not let it go to seven. . . ."

There is another long period of utter silence. I can hear loud talk, sudden laughter from the other locker room. The visitors are arriving. I can hear the locker boy padding across the room alongside me, undoubtedly bringing another hot towel to Rams. I can hear Rams sigh softly as he applies it. "We got to end it right here tonight," Rams says. "Anything can happen in the seventh. . . ."

Frank Ramsey was an All-American at Kentucky University under Adolph Rupp. Auerbach very slyly drafted him, along with Cliff Hagan, a year before they graduated because he alone, among NBA coaches, had somehow figured out that according to the NBA rules they were draftable. After Rams' freshman year, he went off to the service, returning at precisely the right time, a week after Bill Russell had joined us. He had gone away a slim, collegiate type and he returned looking like a testimonial to army food. After the weight came off, he always seemed to have a pale, dumpy, unathletic look about him on the basketball court. Nothing can be further from the truth. Rams is a killer. He has been, for us, the ideal sixth man, the man who has come in to break

things wide open. He is the best substitute—by acclamation—in the history of basketball.

In many ways, he breaks all the rules. At 6'3", he could have very easily been one of the players who gets caught in the middle: too small—far too small these days—to play forward, and not quite quick or nimble enough to play the backcourt. In point of fact, he plays both positions, and plays them exceedingly well. If there is another 6'3" forward in the league, he has escaped my attention. In a few years, 6'3" is going to be too small to make it as a guard.

Here again we see one of the hidden assets of having Bill Russell on your side. With Russell under there to control the boards, Rams can play against those 6'7" forwards, who would ordinarily overpower him. It is not necessary for Rams to battle them under the boards, all he has to do is box his man out for a second or two. Since Russell is also there to help out when the big man tries to take Rams into the pivot, he is more than able to offset the disadvantage in height through his aggressiveness and his quickness.

And Ramsey happens to be a very good rebounder, probably the best rebounder for his size in the league. He is tremendously aggressive and he knows how to use his body.

One of the most honored clichés of basketball is that position is as important to rebounding as jumping ability. That's only part of it, though. The most important part of rebounding is body control. Common sense tells you that even if you have position, a man who is 3 or 4 inches taller—or can simply outjump you—can reach over your shoulder and take the rebound away. He can do it, that is, if you are standing up straight.

So you don't stand up straight. What you do is spread yourself out, pushing your legs apart, bending over slightly and pushing out your rear. Now, if the man behind you wants to stay on your shoulder, he is forced to bend over in exactly the same way. Once you have him in that position he has no traction. It becomes impossible for him to jump. You still have your traction, though, because all you have to do is buff off him as you start to rise, just as if you were in the water with a solid tranchion at your rear. It's as simple as that.

The most difficult thing for any athlete to do is to come into a game cold. This is especially true in basketball, where you have to work right into the pattern. Nobody ever adjusted himself to this role better than Rams. Rams could come into the game and immediately start running and shooting as if he had been playing for 20 minutes. It came to be almost a ritual for me to feed Ramsey as soon as we got possession of the ball, so much of a ritual that our fans came to expect it, and Rams himself began to be a little superstitious about it. And he'd never miss. I'm not saying he hit 90 percent of those first shots; I'm saying the man never missed. All right, almost never!

In addition to everything else, he gives you a good, strong defense. He's aggressive, he has quick enough hands, and he steals a lot of balls.

Most of all, he is a great clutch player. For four straight years, Rams came up with almost unbelievable playoff series. In 1959, when we defeated Syracuse in a tough 7-game series and then swept Minneapolis for the championship, he averaged 23.2 points per game as a sub, playing only about half the game.

Rams is also a solid and dependable man off the court, the kind of person who can always be counted upon to do what's expected of him, to hold up his end. If the wife of one of the players is sick, Frank will be the first guy to go around and say, "Look, let's kick in and send her flowers." For the last couple of years he has spent most of his spare time as a volunteer social worker with the city's Youth Activities Bureau. At his own request, he was assigned to an interracial district.

With it all, he's a careful and conservative businessman. Rams will probably make a million dollars before he's through, and he'll quite probably die with it. During the off-season he has his own construction business in Kentucky. He works at it 14 to 16 hours a day, because he is the kind of man who leaves nothing to chance. He plans everything with meticulous care, putting it all down on paper to make sure it is precise and correct. Rams is the man we all consult on the tax laws, because he has studied them as carefully as any accountant and knows them cold.

The only trouble with Rams is that he becomes as moody as hell when he's playing badly. You think I'm bad? Compared to Frank Ramsey, I'm the life of the party. When Frank is going bad or when he's hobbled by an injury, he is simply not fit to live with.

Last year, he had the kind of season that could have set an optimist to brooding. At the start of the season, he injured his knee so badly that he had to wear an elastic bandage extending all the way from the ankle to the thigh, with only a cutout at the knee to give him flexibility. By midseason, the skin looked like raw beef. Just to look at it as he was dressing made you wince. He had a fair enough year anyway, and he was having his usual good playoffs until the knee collapsed on him again. The last two games against Los Angeles, he just limped up and down the floor, contributing almost nothing. But he wanted to play and despite the tightness of that series Auerbach put him in—solely, I'm sure, as an inspiration to the rest of us. I can remember sitting on the bench while I was resting, watching Rams drag that leg and feeling so bad for him that I could have cried.

Ramsey wanted to retire at the end of last year too, but Walter Brown and Arnold asked him to come back and, like me, he felt a very strong affection for them.

It was a mistake. Although the knee was somewhat stronger, he was never without some kind of an injury. It ate him up so badly that he would go for weeks without talking to anyone. Before the game, he would just sit in his corner and brood, silent and withdrawn. After the game, he would be the first man in the shower, the first man dressed and the first man gone. A group of us who live along Route 9, the highway between Boston and Worcester, would usually stop on the way home for a quick drink, a sandwich and the usual postmortems. Rams didn't stop off to meet us once all year. When we were traveling, he'd sit on the plane by himself, either sleeping or reading.

In the playoffs, where he usually shines, he had been going badly. In that last game in Boston, he had played only 4 minutes; Arnold had preferred to send Havlicek in to pick us up, even though John was limping around on a bad ankle.

The saddest part of it is that while he is basically a solemn person, he's also a congenial guy. Suffering is not really his line.

I know that Walter and Red have asked him to come back again next year and, to be honest, I have advised Rams that it would be the worst thing he could possibly do. I don't doubt he can play another year. I know how important it is to him to go out with a good year, not a bad one. At the same time he's fighting the odds. Looking at it realistically, his chances of having another bad year are much better at this point than his chances of having a good one. He's a man who demands more than just a good year for himself, anyway; he demands perfection. There's no reason for him to subject either himself or his wife to another year like this one.

But now Rams and I are just waiting for the clock to go around. From the main locker room, I can hear the voice of singer Johnny Mathis, who has dropped by to visit Bill Russell. Russell and Mathis were classmates in high school, and they are needling each other about the old school days. Johnny is really coming on strong, and Russ, whose high, cackling laugh has been known to blow down weakly constructed walls, is giving it back in kind.

If you were to watch Russ in the locker room before a game you would think you were seeing a man completely free of any kind of tension. He sings and he laughs and he jokes. He likes to play poker with his buddies, the Jones boys and Sanders, needling them and anybody else who comes under his guns with a loud and wry and very funny barrage of comments. At first, I had the feeling that Arnold didn't like all that kidding around, and on a college level I know I wouldn't like it. From the minute my kids get into the locker room, I'm going to insist that they start concentrating on the game they're about to play. But on a pro level, with the monotony of game after game, you can't possibly expect everybody to handle the problem of building himself up for each game in the same way.

This is Russell's way. Underneath the laughter there's a turmoil inside him. During Arnold's pre-game talk, Russ is going to run to the toilet—*at least once*—to throw up. This is not a prediction in the sense that I'm guessing what will probably happen. Russell is going to throw up—period. I know it, he knows it, everyone knows it. In seven years, Russ has never gone into an important game without throwing up.

On the court, Russell is the man who makes us go. Without him we never won a championship. With him we have won seven straight division championships. We have won the league championship five times and are on our way to our sixth. The one year we lost, Bill was injured in the third game of the final playoff series against St. Louis and while we didn't exactly fall apart, we lost the two final games, 102-100, and 110-109. With Russ in the lineup, you don't lose those close, important games because Russ will always be there to get you the rebound you need.

The basic reason Russell made us go is fairly obvious. We always had a team that was able to shoot, but when your offense is predicated on the fast break and you can't get the rebound, you haven't got a fast break.

Our center had been Ed Macauley, who could score the points and handle the ball. Ed was limited defensively, however. He only stood about 6'8", which wasn't quite big enough even in those days. Worse than that, he only weighed about 180 pounds, and he simply couldn't take the battering under the boards.

There is a story behind the signing of almost all our players. Having finished with the second-best record in the NBA during Bill's senior year at San Francisco U., the Celtics had the No. 7 pick on the draft. Rochester had the first pick and St. Louis the second. Walter Brown had an excellent relationship with Les Harrison, the Royals' owner, partly because Walter had arranged for Les to promote the very profitable ice show at the Rochester stadium. That put Walter in a position to ask Harrison whom he intended to draft. Normally an owner won't give that kind of information to another owner, but Harrison told him that he didn't feel he could compete with the Harlem Globetrotters, who were making a lot of noise about signing Russell. Rochester, he said, was going to take Si Green.

Ed Macauley had already served notice that he was going to retire unless he was traded to St. Louis, his hometown. So Brown offered Macauley and Cliff Hagan to the Hawks for their first draft choice.

There was still one hurdle that had to be overcome. The NBA has a rule that prohibits the trading of draft choices without permission from the rest of the league. At the draft meeting at Leone's restaurant in New York, the other owners agreed that it was a deal that would strengthen both clubs and would therefore be good for the whole league. The year was 1956, and it was, of course, an Olympic year. Both Russ and K. C. Jones were on the Olympic basketball team, which meant he not only couldn't play for us until he came back from Australia, but that, theoretically, he couldn't even think of becoming a professional, a bit of nonsense which both Russell and Walter Brown will readily admit

was not quite observed in the true amateur spirit as laid down by Avery Brundage.

As for the players, we were all aware that if Russell lived up to his reputation, he would supply that ingredient we had always lacked, a man who could control the backboard. At the same time, it was a considerable risk for Brown, because there have been a lot of men who have come into this league with enormous reputations and then disappeared without a trace. The first game Russell played was a nationally televised game against St. Louis—and Macauley—and it was evident from the start that he could do the job defensively.

The only thing that worried us was that it was also evident that he was a poor shooter. A shooting touch is something you either have or don't have. Not all the practice sessions in the world can help you develop it.

On the other hand, as I pointed out to Russ many times in those early years, a pivot man doesn't have to have a shooting touch. From that position, scoring is as much a matter of moving in the proper direction as of shooting. And the proper direction is right into the basket.

There are many players who prefer to avoid contact. Bob Houbregs used to get the ball in the pivot position, take two dribbles out toward the corner and then take a long, sweeping hook shot on which he was fantastically accurate. The only trouble was that he was making an 18- to 20-foot shot out of what could just as easily have been a layup.

A Russell or a Chamberlain, starting from that same position can, with one giant step, go into the hoop, leap, and find himself looking right down into the hole.

Although the Celtics are a fast-break team, we do have seven or eight set plays, which either I or some other guard will call by holding up the indicated number of fingers as we start up the floor. Russell's play is the 3-play.

As the guard comes down with the ball, Russell comes up to a high-post position on the foul line. Assuming I'm the man with the ball, I pass it in to Russ as soon as I pass the half-court line and cut off toward the baseline, bringing my man with me. Sam Jones cuts across as if we're going into a standard crisscross pattern, but Russ doesn't give him the ball, and Sam keeps going, bringing his man away from the middle too. Meanwhile, Sanders has cut under the basket, from left to right, clearing out the whole left side.

As Sam clears past him, Russ turns around on the foul line, facing his man. If the man has not come up to get him, Russ has a 15-foot shot.

The first option, though—the play we want—assumes his man has come up to guard him in the normal way. With the left side cleared out for him, Russ, who is left-handed, fakes and drives around his man for the easy layup.

Now, as the game progresses, I will find that as Russ leaves his position under the hoop to come up to the high post, his man, anticipating the play, begins to follow close up behind him, hoping to jump out in front of him as I throw that long pass and either steal the ball or deflect it. From my position, moving toward them, I can very easily see when that is happening, and when I feel the moment has arrived, I call our next option, which we call the 3-New York, since we first started to use it against New York when Harry Gallatin began to overplay Russell.

There are no rules about how I call it, just so long as Russell gets the message. I may whisper "New York" to him as I pass him at the foul line. If I see the opposing center primed to make his move, after I've called the play coming up the floor, I'll just pump my arm back or turn my palm over, to indicate to Russ that the reverse is on. After you've played together as long as Russ and I, you can practically tell what the other man means when he blinks his eyes at you.

Russ comes up quickly just as before, throws a good fake toward the foul line and, as his man jumps in front of him, he retreats back to the hoop. I throw a high lob pass above the basket, and all Russ has to do is catch it as he leaps and jam it right down through the hoop.

The reason this is a particularly good play for Russell is that his man doesn't even have to jump in front of him. Russ and I are working with a big, relatively awkward man, after all, and once he's committed himself in one direction, he can't recover quickly enough to do anything. Not quickly enough, certainly, to deal with Russell, because Russ is the quickest big man in the league.

There is one point to emphasize. We don't mind the other team knowing what our play is at all, that's why we flash it so openly. In every instance, *we have an option set up—in the event the man is overplayed—that is better than the original play itself.* In other words, we want the defensive man to overplay him.

Other teams have set plays without options, and so you guard against them. Larry Costello, who always makes life so miserable for me, had a beautiful play he was murdering me with. Larry would come upcourt with me guarding him, and when he got a little past the half-court line, he'd pass crosscourt to the other guard, which would automatically make me relax for a second. Kerr, their center, would come up to the high post and he'd take the pass from the other guard, who would follow in right behind his pass, making me think for a moment that he and Kerr were going to set up a double pick for somebody.

That leads me to start falling back, and at this point Larry would begin to move nonchalantly toward the center, making me fall back even more because I'm now anticipating that he's going to cut off the pivot. What I don't know yet is that the Syracuse forward on our side of the court has cut over to the other side, clearing out that whole area behind me. Larry suddenly reverses directions and streaks straight in. To make the play impossible to stop, especially with a man who can fly like Larry, Kerr—without turning—bounces the pass between his legs and Larry is up for an easy layup.

Well, they worked that on me for about three straight times before I got wise and began to look for it. It's a beautiful play if you have a fast man, and I'm going to use it at Boston College.

With Russell, though, anybody who follows basketball knows that his value is not in his scoring but in his defense.

And it isn't simply a matter of taking rebounds, either. Chamberlain not only averages almost three times as many points per game as Russ, he also averages two or three more rebounds. And yet, every year when the players vote on the Most Valuable Player, Russell wins overwhelmingly.

Chamberlain can't understand why he's criticized. Chamberlain is always asking his friends what the hell more people want

from him. Well, it's a question of what you contribute that isn't in the statistics. Basketball is a team game. When it becomes a one-man operation, as it did after Chamberlain came to Philadelphia, it just doesn't work. You cannot expect nine other guys to completely submerge themselves and their abilities to one man. It particularly doesn't work when the man everybody else is feeding isn't helping the others out whenever and wherever he can.

What happens is that Chamberlain scores an unbelievable amount of points—yet his team doesn't even make the playoffs. Next year, Alex Hannum is going to coach the Warriors, and Hannum is a man who demands teamwork. It will be most interesting to see what changes he makes in the offense.

Russell, as everyone knows, is first and foremost a team man. Still, there have been intimations in the press, from time to time, that Russ and I weren't getting along too well because he resented my publicity, my endorsements and my position with the team. Nothing could be further from the truth. Actually it could have been a very ticklish situation if Russ had been a different kind of man, because a player who comes onto a team with his reputation and delivers the way he delivered could very easily throw his weight around. Especially since Russell, in addition to everything else, is a natural leader.

I was captain of the team, I was the playmaker (which made me a sort of quarterback) and I was, even then, the senior player on the team. I was accustomed to expressing my opinions, and Arnold had given me considerable leeway.

What was involved, then, was a question of each us using a little good will and common sense. It was up to me to pass on whatever information or instruction I thought he might be able to use, but to do it constructively, in a way that showed I respected his ability and his own position with the team. As for Russ, he was always more than willing to defer to my position and my seniority. When it's put down this way, it looks more conscious than it was, it looks almost like a negotiated peace. It wasn't like that at all, though. There was simply no friction between us, ever. Nothing was really involved after all, except simple human relations. Russ happens to be very sensitive to the nuances of human relations, and I think I am too.

All this has been leading up to an example I want to give to show how completely Russ is always willing to help out where

98

he is asked to and, in the process, to show something of what makes him so valuable to us.

We all know by now that I have my troubles with Larry Costello. He's so much quicker and faster than I am that the proper way for me to play him is to give him a little room, which means I am conceding him the outside shot. But there are nights when Larry is bombing that hoop from outside, and there are also nights when I'm so worked up that I don't want to give away anything.

Now, when Larry sees me playing him tight, he's going to drive on me. He's going to get that half-step on me without any difficulty, and all I can do is race in after him and try to bother him as much as possible. Two things are now happening. Costello is driving in for soft layups, and I'm knocking the hell out of myself.

But let's not forget that Bill Russell is on my side. I go to Russ and I say, "Look, I'll follow him in as far as I can, and if you see he's by me, come over and help." Now when I see that Larry is by me, I don't bother following him in. Instead, I let him go and start moving the other way. If Russell blocks Larry's shot or bothers him enough so that he misses, the ball is kicked out to me, and I'm already about 15 feet upcourt. I'm not chasing Larry anymore, he's chasing me.

That's what I mean when I say that Russell is always willing to help out. Another man might say, or at least think, "I'm playing 48 minutes and you're playing about 24. I'm running from one end of the court to the other and you're running from foul line to foul line. Why should I do your work for you?"

Russ helps everyone out that way. Just think of the psychological effect on the man who fights past his own man and then finds Russ leaping over to bat the shot right back down his throat. What happens with Costello by now is that after he gets by me he doesn't even try to go in for the layup. He'll stop and take a 15-foot jump shot. His speed, which is his greatest asset, has been completely negated.

This is what Russ has done. He's changed the whole pattern of play, both for teams and for individuals. I've had many guys tell me—and this is absolutely true—that they have nightmares about him. "God," they say, "I wake up at night in a sweat and I see this big black hand hanging over me." He's got the whole league psyched. I know exactly how they feel, because I feel the same way when Chamberlain does it to me. The difference is that, with

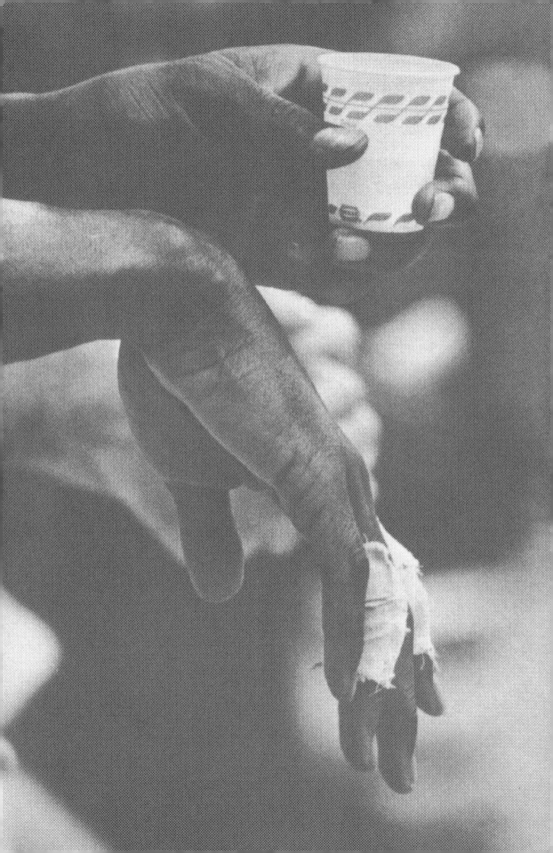

Chamberlain, it only happens when he finds himself near the play. He doesn't help out the way Russ does.

I don't want to be too hard on Wilt. I'm not saying that he isn't great, I'm saying that he could be so much greater. Much of his difficulty, I think, comes down to the psychology of the big man.

A big man tends to be lazy, in the sense that from the time he first picks up a basketball he has such a tremendous advantage over his opponents. In high school and in college he doesn't really have to work to dominate any game he is in. It's like a miler in a race. If nobody ever pushes him, he's never going to run as fast as he can.

There's also the mere fact of their bigness in a culture that roots for the underdog and the little man. They become so self-conscious about hurting a smaller man through the use of their superior height and strength that they become conditioned very early in life to holding something back. They've been made to seem so freakish, even in their own eyes, that they almost seem to be apologizing for being so big.

Then all of a sudden they're playing in the NBA and they haven't got things their own way anymore.

The two most notable exceptions are Bill Russell and George Mikan. Nobody has ever worked any harder than those two. You will notice, though, that neither Russell nor Mikan was a star in high school. They tell me that when George was a sophomore in college he was still so uncoordinated that he had trouble walking up and down the floor, much less running. The coordination came to him all at once, and by then he was accustomed to the long, hard grind.

Russell, as incredible as it seems, couldn't make the *junior varsity* basketball squad when he was a junior in high school, and his record as a senior was fairly undistinguished. Even at San Francisco U., where he finally came into such prominence, it was his ability at defense—which calls for hard work and complete concentration—that was his real forte.

Russ is still at his best when he has to rise to a challenge. He has played better defensive ball against Chamberlain every year Wilt has been in the league, even though, overall, Wilt has been improving every year too. He has studied Wilt so well, and he is able to move so quickly, that Wilt finds it impossible to fake him

101

out. There were full games this season where Wilt never once went into the basket against Russ. He simply gave up and contented himself with taking that fallaway jump shot of his. Now, Wilt is going to hit with that often enough to score his 35 points or so even on a bad night. The point is that Wilt is obviously most effective when he's going into the basket, because even if he misses he has 7'1" of muscle to follow up for a second shot. Neither Russell nor anybody else is going to stop him from scoring, but when Russ forces him to rely exclusively on a shot where he's going away from the basket, he's doing as much as anybody humanly can.

He shoots better against Wilt than against anybody else, because he has to arch the ball higher just to get it over Wilt's head, and that automatically gives him a softer shot. Against the others, he always seems to revert to hard line-drives. Arnold is always telling him, "Why the hell don't you shoot the way you do against Chamberlain? Shoot that way against these other guys and you'd be scoring a lot of points."

With Russell, there is also another more important issue goading him on. Russ is in a turmoil over the postion of the Negro in this country. He would like to tear the social structure of the country apart and he can only tear things apart on the basketball floor. Russ is a crusader. He'd like to make the world better, not only as far as his race is concerned, but as far as everything and everybody is concerned.

I can sympathize with him on two counts. Projecting myself in his place, I know I would feel exactly the same way if I were a member of a minority group and had been humiliated and restricted by prejudice all my life. You just don't say, "All right, I'm a big boy now, I'm a success. I'll forget it."

I can sympathize with him too because I know that crusaders are doomed to disappointment and disillusionment.

Russ feels that since he is a Negro in the public eye he should be doing more in the whole area of civil rights. At the same time he feels that playing basketball is, essentially, a waste of time, and that if he were in a somewhat more important field he would be able to do much more.

Before the season opened in 1961, the Celtics went to Louisville to play the St. Louis Hawks in an exhibition game in honor

102

of Frank Ramsey and Cliff Hagan. The Celtics will not go any-where unless we can all stay together and eat together, and I'm sure every other team has the same policy. The policy of the hotel in Louisville was that if a Negro was registered at the hotel he would be served at the coffee shop, but that if he walked in off the street he would not be. Which in itself is not the greatest ex-ample of democracy in action you have ever heard of.

Sanders and Sam Jones went to the coffee shop, and the waitress, assuming that they had come in off the street, refused to serve them. Well, Russell has passed the point where he will submit himself to any kind of indignity, and he immediately told Auerbach that they were leaving. I had gone somewhere with a friend of mine, and by the time I returned to the hotel they were all on the plane and out of there.

I thought they did exactly the right thing. I've had arguments about it with several people, including a couple of referees, who argued bitterly that they had "only thought of themselves" in-stead of the image of the league. Well, if they don't think of them-selves, I don't know who else is going to.

It's so easy to sit back and take that reasoned, objective view when it's somebody else's dignity being affronted. I remember once in Charlotte I was getting my shoes shined. Sitting next to me was a well-dressed elderly man. When the shoe-shine boy, a colored kid of about twelve or thirteen, was finished, this nice, pleasant-looking man went into his pocket, took out fifteen pennies and flung them down at his feet. Just flung them down as if the kid were dirt. You can read a hundred articles about it and talk about it all night, but when you see it in action you are never quite prepared for the shock.

And I can remember when Chuck Cooper, the first Negro in the league, found he wasn't going to be allowed to stay in the hotel with us in Raleigh, N. C., or eat with us, or go to the movies with us. Chuck had been brought up in Pittsburgh, attended college at Duquesne, and he had never been exposed to that kind of thing before. He was a good-looking boy, and a man of class, intelli-gence and sensitivity. Visibly shaken, he decided to get out of town as quickly as possible.

Chuck and I had roomed together on the road, and we had be-come very close. Not wanting to see him leave alone, I asked

Arnold for permission to go with him. We arrived at the train station at 2 A.M. to catch the night sleeper. You're there in a train station, practically alone, and suddenly you become aware of the signs that say WHITE and COLORED. We couldn't enter the waiting room or the coffee shop by the same door. Theoretically, we couldn't drink from the same water fountain.

It becomes one of those situations where you're embarrassed without reason. The last thing in the world you want is for him to think you're patronizing him, and yet the whole atmosphere around you is trying to shout at both of you that you are. Jeez, the thing that upsets me even more than prejudice is to hear people talk about being *tolerant*. To me, it's a word that carries the connotation that you have the *right* to be tolerant of somebody else. Especially since it's usually being used by some sanctimonious bastard who's saying, "I'm as tolerant as the next guy, but . . ." Where does one man get the presumption to be tolerant of another man. Tolerant of *what*, his right to be alive?

To break through that sudden feeling of embarrassment and, I suppose, to prove to Chuck that I was sharing the experience with him, not just observing it, I found myself saying that, well . . . they had been throwing bombs in Catholic churches down South too. And I'll never forget Chuck looking at me and saying, "The only trouble with that is you can't tell by looking at someone whether he's a Catholic or not."

So I don't have too much patience with those guys who think the "image" of the league, whatever that means, is more important than one man's image of himself. I don't think that, in practice, there are any racial barriers in the NBA, although you do hear whispering about a color quota having been set to achieve what is usually referred to as "a balance." I suspect that the owners do sit around and talk about limiting the squads to, say five Negroes, but the competition is so rough that when it comes down to it, they sign the guy who can do them the most good.

I do know one thing. I have never seen or heard of one incident among the players in the thirteen years I've been in this league. That's why I opened my big mouth when Chamberlain wrote that article at the end of his first year, in which he announced he was quitting and cited the abusive treatment he had received as one of the reasons. It seemed to me that he was implying there was prejudice among the players, and I couldn't let that kind of imputation go unchallenged.

There are some Boston sportswriters who look upon Russell as a surly, uncooperative guy, because if Russ, with that sensitive antenna of his, picks up waves that tell him you are no friend of his, he can be completely unapproachable. But if he feels a rapport with a writer he can be exactly the opposite. Basically, he is a witty man, a lover of music, a good companion.

While Ramsey and I are waiting to be called into the front locker room, Tommy Heinsohn wanders into the back locker room to join us. We now have a real normal human being in among us pallbearers. This close to the game, though, there's no kidding around on Tommy's part either. He's drawn and tense. "Let's end it right here," he says. "Now. Tonight."

"Yeah," Ramsey says, "let's not let it go to the seventh game."

"Yeah," I say, "anything can happen in the seventh game. There's no coming back from that seventh game."

"We got to expect them to play real tough defense tonight," Tommy says. "That's how they beat us in Boston."

"We got to keep running," I say. "We got to move. All the time."

Twenty minutes before game time, Arnold sends the locker boy in to summon us to the meeting. The pre-game instructions are about to commence. Most teams allow themselves 20 minutes to warm up out on the floor. We usually content ourselves with 15 minutes.

The kidding has stopped now. Everybody is seated on his locker-room chair, drawn out slightly to form a rough semicircle around Arnold. Buddy LaRoux is alongside John Havlicek, because John has been his special project this past week.

Havlicek is in his rookie year, and a very pleasant surprise he has been. John had played with Jerry Lucas at Ohio State, and he was more or less lost in Lucas' publicity. Actually, Cincinnati, who took Lucas as its territorial choice, was confident Havlicek would still be there when it came around to them again. Red took him, I think, mostly because of that affection of his for the player who has grown accustomed to winning.

John is 6'5", strong and raw-boned. Like Ramsey, he can play both the frontcourt and backcourt. Like Ramsey, he's always hustling and gets the most out of his ability.

John Havlicek, by himself—by professional standards—isn't that good a player. But when you put him in with the Celtics, and use his specialized talents, he becomes one hell of a player. Here you have the value of Russell again. John came to us as a forward, and we could afford to take a calculated gamble with him, despite his size, because there was no pressure on him to get his share of rebounds. (Although once he got some experience under his belt, he turned out to be an excellent rebounder and a strong defensive player. That's just the point, though. With another team, he would never have got the chance, or the pressure would have been on him to produce at once or go home.)

He's not a great shooter by any means, either, maybe a little better than adequate. But he picks up a lot of garbage baskets with that second and third effort, and after Arnold had worked him into the backcourt, he was frequently playing against smaller men whom he could overpower on sheer strength and hustle.

He's going to improve too. There's no doubt in my mind about that. For one thing, his shooting is going to improve as he picks up confidence and learns to take better-percentage shots. For another thing, he's got the right attitude. It has been a long time since I've seen a rookie with his fierce desire to win. I don't have to tell you by now how annoying it is to come into a locker room after you've been bombed and see these guys clowning around and laughing. Havlicek goes to his locker and he sits there, and he drops his head, and when he does begin to talk it's to replay the game to find out where it went wrong, and most particularly to replay his own mistakes.

Right from the beginning, he was very popular with the rest of the players. He took his rookie hazing in good spirit. He's completely unaffected, with no visible complexes of any kind. Just a good, normal college kid.

In the first game of the Laker series, John injured his ankle chasing a ball over the bench and it blew up like a balloon. When I first saw it after the game, I never thought he'd get back in. I'd never seen an ankle that bad.

The schedule helped him, though. We had three days off between the first two games in Boston and the second two games in

L. A., another three days before the fifth game in Boston, and three more before this one tonight in L. A. So, actually, John missed only two complete games. He's been playing at less than full speed, though, no doubt about that. When you have a man whose main asset is his continual all-around hustle, he isn't going to help you too much if he's favoring one leg.

John has moved in with Buddy over the past week and they've been together constantly, going through all kinds of special exercises and treatment. Arnold seems satisfied that he's ready.

"Well, has everyone gone to the head?" Arnold is saying. "Has everyone been taped? Has everybody taken care of all their problems so we can get this meeting started?"

Now Arnold is all business. There's no pep talks with professionals, never anything about going out to do or die for the dear old Celtics. Pros are pretty sophisticated about this kind of thing.

Knute Rockne would be laughed right out of town. A basketball team consists of a small group of men. The nucleus remains together for years. A coach would make himself ridiculous trying to work you up through pep talks.

The pre-game talk is a matter of going over our assignments, and even here we are facing a team we have already faced five straight times. He can only remind us of specific things to be alert for. Watch for this. Let's be careful of that. Force the ball here.

There's no special basketball jargon used. There's not a word that wouldn't be understood by even a casual basketball fan. Lately, I've been going around talking to college coaches, and I find those boys are developing a specialized vocabulary of pure unadulterated jargon. Pretty soon they'll be sounding like football coaches. I've been playing the game for twenty-five years, and half the time I can't understand what they're talking about.

The only time for a pep talk, really, is between halves. I've been thinking about this lately in relation to my own locker-room talks at Boston College. I'm sure that even on a college level the boys themselves generate enough spirit at the start of the game to carry them out there. It's only between halves, if they haven't been playing well, it seems to me, that their morale would need bolstering. Looking back over the years, I'm sure Auerbach has worked on this theory. If you're 20 points ahead at halftime, any kind of pep talk becomes superfluous and Arnold just doesn't bother. It's in a close game, where we've been playing rather poorly, that he'll try to jazz us up. Even here Arnold leans more to scorn than to inspiration, and he has never been known for the modesty of his vocabulary.

That isn't it really, either, Arnold gets so mad that he just bursts in and raises hell. It's his emotion that moves you, not his words. Thinking back, I wonder if we even hear what he's saying. Silence can be emotional under certain circumstances too. A coach's silence can be more stirring than a 20-minute lecture.

Arnold seldom resorts to silence. Arnold is a man who comes in and breaks things. "What the hell's going on?" he'll scream. "What do you think this is, a prom or something?" When a coach is really angry, you know it's genuine, and his emotion permeates the room. The players get mad either at him or at themselves—it

108

doesn't matter which—and they go back out there in just the mood they ought to be in. But you can't fake it. You can't even get mad too often, I would suppose, or the law of diminishing returns sets in.

There's nothing new and startling for Arnold to tell us at this point, and yet the repetition of the old familiar tactics relaxes you and keys you up at the same time. You're finally getting into it. The waiting has come to an end.

The main point Arnold is emphasizing is that we must keep LaRusso and Baylor off the boards. "If we keep those two guys off," he says, "Russell is going to be able to control the defensive boards with no trouble at all. The only time Russ can get into trouble is when we let those two get in there, and he gets hammered from all angles."

The techniques to be used on LaRusso and Baylor are entirely different. What Heinsohn has to do is to wheel around and box La-Russo out, since LaRusso will come in facing him. Baylor will do that too, but more often than not he will be bulling his way to the basket with his back to Satch Sanders.

The Lakers' strategy is to clear one side so that Baylor can go to work on his man in a one-on-one situation. Starting from either the corner or the high-post, Elgin will drive in as far as he can and then put his back to Satch and start working his way into the basket on a combination of brute strength and maneuverability. Once he has worked his way in close enough he has only to spin around and jump and he's in there for an easy basket. Satch's defense is to try to plant his feet firmly and more or less shove his forearm into Elgin's back to hold him off and still be ready to move in either direction when Elgin makes his move.

If only it were that easy. To begin with, it's almost impossible to lean into him like that and not foul him when he wheels and jumps, which means that at worst Elgin gets two foul shots, both of which he will probably make, and at best he sinks the basket and has a 3-point play. And just to give Sanders something else to think about in case it gets boring for him out there, if Elgin misses the shot and is not fouled he'll still be up there for the rebound because he's quicker than anybody else that tall (6'5") and he's stronger than any other 225-pounder. Pound for pound, he's so strong that he simply overpowers anyone who tries to guard him.

I would say that Baylor's second and third efforts, from outside as well as inside, are so powerful that they comprise 60 percent of his game. As long as I'm praising him, I might as well mention the part of his game that most impresses everybody, players and fans alike. Big as he is, Elgin has a way of hanging in the air as if the law of gravity had not yet been discovered, twisting and turning up there to evade the men who have jumped with him, and still maintaining complete control of the ball to the very last second. He's really an acrobat and a strong man combined.

The guy is just unstoppable—period. In many respects, I think he's as effective offensively as Chamberlain, even though Chamberlain scores more points. There's no question at all that Elgin gets much more out of his ability than Wilt does.

His rebounding is tremendous too. He leads the Lakers in rebounding, in fact, although that's partly because the Lakers have not had a good big man to take some of the pressure off him. His passing, while not spectacular, is good. If a man is open or someone is being double-teamed, Elgin will see it immediately and hit the right man with his pass. He also throws the difficult long pass very well.

His defense, while below the rest of his game, is certainly adequate. With his speed and reflexes I suspect he could play a real strong defense if it weren't necessary for him to conserve his energy on some part of his game. In other words, when you talk about forwards, you have to start with Elgin Baylor.

Offense is where he kills you, though, inside or out. He is the only guy I ever saw who was able to improve one of his shots— in his case, his outside shot—so much from one year to the next that he upgraded himself from an excellent player to a super player.

In his first two years in the league, I considered Baylor a good shooter from the outside but hardly an exceptional one. And then he came back, the following year, with a fantastic one-hand shot. Elgin just holds the ball over his head, 18 to 22 feet from the basket, and his wrists are so strong that if you don't come up on him he can snap the shot off without bringing his hand down a fraction of an inch. And that goes for both the stationary one-hander and the jumper.

This means that if you are guarding him, you have to go out to him and cover him very closely. The only trouble then is that his reflexes are so fantastic and his first step so lightning quick, that once you go out to him he can drive by you to either his left or his right.

If you can't lay back and you can't move up, the only thing left, it would seem, is to stay on him closely at all times, first to try to keep him from getting the ball (the best idea of all), but mostly to cut down the percentages on the jump or the drive. This is how Sanders does play him. After a while—especially when you are playing the same man in a long series—you get to know his moves and his fakes and his drives well enough so that you can do a halfway decent job on him. With Elgin, if you do an exceptionally good job and he isn't feeling well, you may hold him to 25 points. You won't do it often. When you play him that close, Baylor starts working you in, one-on-one, a beautiful sight to behold if you're up in the stands watching him instead of down on the floor playing against him. I know this sounds ridiculous, and yet it's the gospel truth: the night Baylor scored 61 points against us, Sanders played a pretty good defensive game.

How, then, can you hope to beat a team that has Elgin Baylor? Well, we have Bill Russell.

And Russ helps out.

At the start of the series, Auerbach has discussed the strategy with Russell, because he respects Russell as one of basketball's keener students of defense. They have agreed that Russell will remain under the boards on defense, and move in to double-team Baylor whenever he starts to work his way in on Sanders on that one-on-one setup. When Baylor starts to wheel, Russ will leap over and try to bat the shot away. We now have the strongest defensive man against the strongest offensive man, and our man has almost 5 extra inches and at least twelve extra hands.

But what is Russell's man doing while Russ is busy with Elgin? The Lakers quite obviously have two options. They can, if they wish, keep him under the board, so that Baylor can pass to him when Rusell goes for Elgin. The only trouble there is that if Russell can block Baylor's shot toward the basket, he can also block a pass under the basket. The percentage strategy for them is to play their center out at the foul line. If Russell goes out to cover him, Baylor is left free to maneuver as he wishes and, with Russell away from the boards both Baylor and LaRusso have a much better chance of getting in for the rebound. That not only gives them

their second effort but negates our fast break.

If Russell still stays under the boards and double-teams Baylor, Elgin now has an easy outlet pass to his center, who has only to pop the ball in from 15 feet away.

The percentage for us, Red and Russ have decided, is to take a chance on letting the Lakers' center take the 15-foot one-hander. Big centers have never been known for their soft touch from outside, with the sole exception of Clyde Lovellette (who is sitting on our bench in case a sudden case of plague hits Russell).

The catch here is that we used the same strategy last year, and Jim Krebs, the Lakers' center, murdered us. Krebs, at 6'8", has always been a run-of-the-court performer. His defense leaves something to be desired and his rebounding isn't any better than it should be for such a comparatively small center. Nor is he any great threat as a scorer.

So in last year's playoffs, Krebs went out, played as good a defense as I've seen from him, rebounded better than he had ever rebounded in his life and, far more important, kept taking Baylor's outlet pass and popping in that one-hander.

He gave them points we hadn't figured on, and he made us change our plans. If Russ stayed in and helped out with Baylor, Krebs hit the outside shot. If Russ went out and smothered Krebs, Baylor ate us up inside. We were caught in the switches.

Krebs had always had a reputation for being a hard man to handle, and it was apparent that Freddie Schaus, in his second year as coach, had nursed him along and gotten more out of him than anyone thought possible. This season, Schaus had been breaking in two tall (6'10") rookie centers, Gene Wiley and LeRoy Ellis.

According to the grapevine, which isn't always reliable, Freddie had been having difficulty with Krebs, possibly—assuming the rumors were true—because Jim was not overjoyed at spending most of his time on the bench. A couple of weeks before the series, Krebs had injured his hand. Still, looking back at last year's playoffs, none of us had doubted for a moment that Jim would be ready for the series and primed to make things rough for us again.

To our astonishment, he had hardly been used at all in the previous five games. Freddie had been trying so hard to bring his kids along through the year that he wouldn't admit to himself that they couldn't do the job. And as far as we were concerned they couldn't. Maybe they'll do it yet, but they had been remarkably unimpressive all year.

This was the break we had never expected to get. It has been the main reason, along with Heinsohn's improved play, that we have been completely dominating this year's series in comparison to last year's.

Wiley, who has been playing twice as much as Ellis, hasn't been able to hit a bull's tail with a handful of buckshot. Not only isn't Russ bothering to go out to cover him—by this time, Russ isn't even bothering to look at him. Ellis has been no better. Between them, they have not been averaging 5 points a game.

Krebs did get into that last Boston game, during that hot streak that won the game, and he had popped in three baskets. Arnold talks it over with Russ, and they decide that Schaus is undoubtedly too committed to Wiley at this point to make a change. If Krebs does start, Russ will still camp under the basket at the beginning of the game and wait to see what happens. If Wiley starts, as anticipated, Russ will, of course, continue to ignore him.

"If those rookies have been feeling the pressure before," Red tells him, "they'll be feeling it more than ever now."

Arnold goes over Sanders' role in this defensive strategy again, in detail. Although Satch has heard it all before, he sits there listening intently, nodding to show he understands. There are some guys who will nod because they don't want to be bothered. There are others who will be argumentative. There are some, like Ramsey, who will set up a little debate simply to have everything spelled out, everything very clear in their mind.

From the beginning of the series, Satch has analyzed every move very closely with Auerbach, examining alternatives and analyzing Baylor's probable reaction to every squeeze we plan to put on him. Nobody on the Celtics is more conscientious about trying to absorb what he is being told. Even more to the point, he goes out to the court and tries to apply whatever tactics have been decided upon. There is frequently a very large gap between the pre-game plan and the actual play. A basketball game can be like a beachhead invasion. The battle plan gets forgotten when the bullets start flying, and sheer reflex action takes over. But not with Satch.

If anything, Satch thinks too much, and that can sometimes be as harmful as not thinking enough. You can't outthink yourself on defense since, as I have said, defense is 90 percent concentra-

tion. Offense is something else again. If Satch misses his first couple of shots, he will usually lose all confidence and just stop shooting. As a result, he scores in spurts. He'll have a good night, and that will encourage him to the point where he'll go along for a week or two giving you 12 or 14 points a game. Then he'll hit a bad night, stop looking, and come up with 4 or 6 points a game.

He isn't a shooting forward in our overall pattern, anyway. He's primarily our defensive forward. He has the tough, thankless job of guarding the Baylors and the Pettits and the Twymans, the rough equivalent of the guard's job in football. He does a much better than adequate job on them, and he also gives you a solid rebounding forward. No matter what kind of a job you do, though, the way these guys can shoot and move, boy, they're going to score. Satch can break his back all night, and the average fan, reading the scoring totals—or even watching the game—will see only that his man has scored 25 or 30 points.

When you have to guard a guy like Baylor for seven games in a pressure series, it must really work on your insides. You're all over him, he's falling on his face, and he still puts the ball in the hole.

Sanders is one of the excellent draft pickups for the Celtics in the last few years. As perennial champions we have had, perennially, the No. 10 choice. The chance of picking up a useful player that far down on the list—unless you have a territorial choice—doesn't figure to be very good. The Knicks could have had Sanders as territorial choice, as far as that goes. Satch is a New York boy and he played for New York University. The Knicks passed him up for a big man, Darrell Imhoff, and Imhoff did nothing for them. Satch has done far more for us than we expected or had any right to hope.

People seem to think Satch is a real hipster, because of that widely publicized greeting to President Kennedy—"Take it easy, Baby."—during a Celtic tour of the White House. But Satch blurted that out out of sheer nervousness. He is a very quiet, conservative, intelligent and sensitive boy—and thoughtful. I once asked him, very casually, to play on a team I was putting together for a charity game in Worcester during one of our off days. Later, he came to me, explained that he had an offer to pick up some money in an exhibition game that same night, but wanted me to know that if I needed him he'd turn it down and come to Worcester. We didn't need him at all, we had plenty of name players. But the way he went about it typifies to me the kind of person he is.

A basketball player's performance on the floor can frequently be a reflection of his personality, especially when you're dealing with a young player. Satch's principal flaw as a player at the moment, his reluctance to push for his own shots, is a perfect reflection of his rather quiet, retiring personality.

Russell jumps up, heading for the toilet across the hall, to throw up. The rest of us take no notice. We're used to it. Auerbach doesn't even miss a beat. A few moments later we hear him throwing up, another sound that has become almost background music to Arnold's instructions.

The locker boy comes in to tell us that the officials are going to be Earl Strom and Norm Drucker. The officials aren't announced beforehand, so you don't know who they are going to be until they go to their own dressing room just before the game. Since to some small extent the officials can influence the type of game you are going to play, it is part of every Locker boy's duties to carry the news to the coach.

While it would be misleading to overstate the importance either the coach or the players place upon the officials, every official, like every player, has his idiosyncrasies, and to some extent you have to observe them and be guided.

Sid Borgia, the supervisor of referees, feels that fouls should not be called unless they are flagrant. It is his theory that the superior referee keeps whistle-blowing down to the absolute minimum consistent with maintaining control of the game. So when the boy comes in and announces that Borgia is working a game, Auerbach will tell our big boys to go out and really knock heads under there. Not only are they going to get away with more contact than would normally be allowed, but if they don't go out prepared to throw their weight around they stand to get the hell knocked out of them.

Arnold is, needless to say, quite pleased when our guy gets away with something, and outraged when the other guy does. This may not sound like either good logic or good democratic practice but it is, without doubt, the sign of a good coach.

I'm somewhat interested in who's going to be working the game myself. If Borgia is officiating, I might be more interested in passing in certain situations than in driving, since there isn't an awful lot to be gained in getting myself racked up if I might not even get a foul shot out of it. As I say, though, it's not anything that changes your basic strategy; it's just something to file away in the back of your mind.

If you draw a new official, especially a young one, he's going to be making every chicken call in the book, because he's apprehensive about letting the game get away from him. So now I adjust the other way. Given the opportunity, I'm going to be driving—and picking up those fouls—all night.

When the players get together and talk about the officials—and you can't get three of us together without the subject coming up—we generally agree that we don't care how much contact they allow as long as they're consistent. The guy who drives you crazy is the one who calls you for something, late in the game, that he hasn't been calling all night.

The other two officials who have been working in the finals are Mendy Rudolph and Dickie Powers, and I realize now that there has been very little said about their work during this series which, according to folklore, is the best compliment they can be paid. The Cincinnati series had been featured by more' moaning and griping, more accusation and recrimination—from both camps—than I had ever heard in my life.

Earl Strom, in my opinion, has been as good an official as we've had in the league this year. Along with Dickie Powers, he calls as tight a game as anybody in the league, although nowhere near as tight as a college official would, but both he and Dickie also call a very consistent game. Strom's only idiosyncrasy is that he'll call a charging foul on a slightly less degree of contact than the average official will. But it is not a difference marked enough to even bother about in your pre-game thinking.

Norm Drucker calls a consistent game too. Norman tries very hard to keep the game under control, which means that if he leans in any direction it is to the tight side. Still, he hardly calls them so tight that you'd list him with Strom or Powers.

The thing you have to remember about Norman is that, more than any other official in the league, he will flare right back at a coach or a player who is giving him a hard time. We players naturally feel that an official should stay above that kind of battle because once he starts to give it back to you, you almost automatically come right back at him again. And that's a battle you can't possibly win, because he has a whistle and all you have is your lungs. You can yell at him, but he can throw you out of the game.

Red, hearing the names of the officials, just shrugs. They can both be pretty much discounted as far as body contact is concerned.

From across the way, we can hear Russ going through the agonies of the dry heaves. There was a time when I used to wonder how the poor guy could go out and play the kind of ball he does after he has been wrenched and racked the way you are after an attack of dry heaves. By now I just take it for granted.

At this point, I, as captain, have a word or two I've been waiting to get in. I want to emphasize that, above all, we want to keep running. "The mistake we made in Boston," I say, "was that we just stood around in the fourth quarter and let them come on. If we get the lead tonight, let's not sit on it. We're a team that has to run, we're geared that way. We've become too accustomed to playing a running game to be effective on a slow-down, deliberate, patterned style of play."

"Right," Arnold says. "Even if we jump off to a 12- or 14-point lead we got to keep running. If we let these guys start to gain momentum on their home court they'll come on like tigers."

One of the most difficult decisions to make in any sport is whether to sit on a lead or to hold to the pace and tempo that has built up the lead in the first place. There's no sport where this is more of a problem than in basketball because there's no other sport where the points come as fast and as furious.

The coach can always protect himself by sitting on the lead, because even if he loses it seems like the logical thing to have done. If he goes all out and blows the lead, everybody's going to second-guess him. You can't tell me the fear of being second-guessed doesn't sit in the back of every coach's mind.

I've been playing this game long enough to have become completely convinced that what seems to be logical isn't. Basketball is more emotional than logical. Because it is a game of emotion, it is also a game of momentum. I've seen too many teams open too many floodgates by sitting on those big leads. I am absolutely convinced that regardless of the size of the lead, the offense has to continue to move, to go for the basket, to keep applying the pressure. In theory, it seems logical to slow the game down and look for the good shot. What happens, psychologically, is that in being so careful you become a little gun-shy and end up missing those good shots you've been waiting for so patiently.

This is the cue for the other team to take heart. They hit a couple of baskets, pick up their own momentum, and almost before you know what has happened your 20-point lead has been washed away.

Unless you have competed in some sport, it's impossible to grasp how important momentum is. And yet, on that court, it can become something so tangible that you can almost cut it with a knife. You've been sitting on the lead, either on instructions from the bench or because a big lead tends to make you cautious—especially away from home—and suddenly you feel this surge coming at you. It's as if you're in the middle of an ocean, bobbing around helplessly. The waves hit you, pass over you, sweep past you, and there's not a thing you can do about it, except to try to hang in there and fight the undertow.

Because once you've lost your momentum, you can't regenerate your rhythm and aggressiveness as an act of will. You run around yelling, "Come on, guys, let's stop them. . . . Let's start running. . . . Let's start moving." Let's do this, you say, let's do that. But words aren't going to help you, because it's emotion that's involved here, not intellect.

And then, just as suddenly, something happens that tells you their momentum has hit its peak and is on the wane. They miss an easy basket or they sink the basket and get a bad call. We come rushing right back to score and we begin to sense that the tide has shifted and we are now riding the wave, not fighting it. We begin to get a little more out of each guy, and it's like a little fire running from one man to the other, a little charge of electricity. This will happen two or three times in a single game, back and forth. I have often said I'd much rather be a few points down at the half, with a running team like the Celtics, because it is the team that gathers this momentum at the end that usually rides it through to victory.

Never underestimate the power of the home crowd to pick you up and sweep you along, for their cheers come at you in waves too. We all have a little bit of ham in us, and the crowd's applause after a good play is exhilarating. The thing that will always arouse me the most, emotionally, is when you are down 8 or 10 points at home and you start coming back, gobbling up their lead—as the crowd goes wild—then finally going ahead. The other team will finally call their time out just as you make that last hoop and, boy, everything explodes at once. You think the roof is going to blow off. The roar in baseball after a home run can't compare with it, because although we have fewer people, our crowd is packed together in a small arena. There's nothing to compare with it, that last loud roar. Nothing!

I know it is going to be difficult for me to leave the competition behind. I've lived with it all my life and thrived on it. I can only hope that the competition inherent in coaching will replace it.

And the cheers will be tough to leave behind too. I imagine that is what actors mean when they talk about the exhilaration they feel when the applause comes up at them from out of the darkness. Say what you want, the applause of the crowd is like a drug: the more you have, the more you want. I do not expect the withdrawal symptoms to be painless.

By this time, it should be apparent that basketball is a game that would have delighted Sigmund Freud, in that it is a game composed in equal parts of muscle, skill and psychology.

In many ways, for instance, basketball players are closer to each other than the players of any other professional sport. You don't get the jockeying you get in baseball, and you don't get anything approaching the organized warfare of hockey. We have explosions and we have fights, but they always come out of the heat of contact and almost never get carried over to the next game.

And yet, as I have been at some pains to show, I have always been able to generate this competitive hatred toward my opponent to the point where once I'm on the court I don't want to have anything to do with the guy. The one thing that has always annoyed me above all others is to see players fraternizing before a game. In the first meeting I have with the kids I'll be coaching, I intend to lay down a flat edict that they are never to fraternize with the opposition.

I can honestly say that there isn't a backcourtman in the league who isn't a friend of mine off the court. Richie Guerin and I have gone on barnstorming tours together. I like him very much and I feel that he likes me. When we are playing against each other, Richie is just another guy in uniform and I hate him. I think of him as my enemy, because that is exactly what he is.

This attitude of implacable hostility is especially important when you are playing on your home court. The home-court advantage you hear so much about is 99 percent psychological. When visiting players come to Boston and see 13,909 screaming fans in the stands, they have to be a little concerned. I know darn well they are, because I'm more than a little concerned when I'm playing on their home court. I'm in the enemy camp. I feel the hostility, and I'm apprehensive.

But I noticed something interesting very early in my career. I noticed that when the guy assigned to guard me came up to me before the game and gave me a nice smile and a lot of pleasant chatter, I would become less concerned, less worried, less vulnerable to my surroundings. I'd start the game much looser, and I'd be much more effective.

Well, I'm not going to give him that welcome feeling when he's in my camp. I'll observe the amenities, which call for me to shake his hand, but you can be sure it will be a very cursory handshake, nothing more really than the touch of hands. I'm not out there to smile and ask him how he's feeling. If I look at him at all, it will be only to scowl.

Does that make him a nicer guy than me? Maybe it does. But when you have two evenly matched teams, as you do in the playoffs, it's just these little things that are going to make the difference. Leo Durocher said it, and he was right. In competitive sports, *nice guys finish last.*

It is just because of this, because basketball is a game of psychology and emotion and momentum, that we can beat the Lakers by 20 points one night and then lose to them by 20 the next. The same people who know very well that they don't go to their office and perform their tasks exactly the same every day expect athletes in a competitive game to be perfectly consistent. And so every year I have to listen to all that garbage about the playoffs always going seven games. The implication being that we are stretching it out deliberately to make sure we rake in all those gate receipts. The fact of the matter is that five of the past eight World Series have gone the full seven games, and only four of the last eight NBA finals.

People can not seem to understand that when two teams are as evenly matched as ourselves and the Lakers, the psychological factors are going to be decisive. The team that can get itself up to the highest competitive pitch, sustain its spirit the longest and exploit the most psychological gambits is going to be the team that wins.

Nobody can question that the home-court advantage in the NBA is purely psychological. The courts are all the same, the baskets are the same, the balls are the same and the teams are the same.

I have already pointed out two of the factors. That roar of the home crowd inspires the home team. The visitors enter with a feeling that may not be exactly trepidation but is, at the very least, concern.

The home team's strongest psychological edge, though, is that it *knows* it has an edge. The fact that we know, from experience and conditioning, that we are starting out with an advantage gives us an even greater advantage.

Playing at home, you're not afraid to make mistakes, because you somehow feel that, having such a strong advantage, you can afford to make mistakes and still have a good chance to win. You're loose and you're easy and instead of making mistakes you make baskets.

Let's look at it in reverse. Knowing that we are at a disadvantage when we are away from home, we feel that any mistake will probably be fatal. We come down the floor and we don't take the same chances, we don't make the same natural moves. Being slightly on the defensive, we tend to become a bit hesitant, a little gun-shy. We're playing "scared," in other words, and the surest way to insure defeat in any competitive sport is to play scared. The attitude is not the same as the attitude of the team that is trying to hold on to a lead by sitting on it, but the result is still the same.

In the first place, when you're playing basketball at this level, the offensive maneuvers I have been describing have, through practice and repetition, become purely automatic. It is not until a move is made automatically, through reflex action, that it becomes part of your repertoire. The man who has to stop and say *Now I will do this*—let alone *Should I do this?*—will not succeed in doing it.

In the second place, if you are afraid to make a mistake you tend to hold back, and that is equally fatal. The accuracy of your shot, to give one example, comes in part from your follow-through. When you are tense or hesitant, you pull the arm back too soon and the ball is going to go off-course and hit the rim. Any golfer or tennis player knows this is true. Hold back on the golf club and you slice the ball. Hold back on your tennis swing, and you'll probably hit the ball on the frame or on the wrist.

I have tried to explain this to fans and I find it's impossible. "What are you talking about?" they say. "You guys are pros, aren't you?" Sure we're pros. But human nature doesn't declare a holiday just because we're getting paid.

Being a pro makes a difference in only one way. Since we are the top ninety players in the country, almost all of us have the physical ability to do almost anything we have confidence we can do. An amateur might have all the confidence in the world, but his chances of succeeding would be slight if his physical abilities were limited.

I have always believed that the officials are also affected by the home crowd. When two players bump under the basket, the call is pure reflex action on his part. Suppose the game were being played at Syracuse, where police protection is—to put it kindly—sparse, and the crowds are so rabid that they have been known to come down after the officials. Now you can not tell me that the officials aren't aware of this—*not consciously, subconsciously*. Not that they're going to give the home team a foul when they need it, or anything like that. It's in the calls of omission rather than commission that it shows up. The foul that is not called immediately is not called at all.

I have tried to discuss this, calmly and sanely, with several officials, and all of them have indignantly denied it. "This doesn't reflect on you," I assure them. "I'm telling you that the same thing would happen to me. It hapens to me just playing. You're a brave and loyal human being, a man of great integrity. I concede that. But subconsciously, this has to be working in the back of your mind, and when you're making instinctive decisions it has to have an effect."

If the officials don't believe they can be influenced, the coaches quite obviously don't agree with them. Working the crowd up against the referee is an art which has been developed to a degree that might appall the more distinguished jurists in the land but which thrills all connoisseurs of free-style rabble-rousing. Our man, Arnold Auerbach, is widely known, for reasons which escape only those who have never seen him in action, as the league-leading referee-baiter—although I'm afraid he's now living off past glories. Arnold has mellowed so much in the last three or four years that there are at least three or four other coaches who are every bit as vehement and vociferous as he.

Arnold operates on the theory that he is never going to get anything he doesn't fight for. He also believes that if you're a nice guy, the officials are not going to give you your due. Arnold will insist, therefore, that we shoot at the basket nearest our own bench at the start of a home game, so that the other team will be shooting at it in the second half. Most fouls occur under the defensive boards, and Arnold wants the officials to be directly under his guns as the game is coming to a close. If his constant complaining, backed and reinforced by the roaring of the crowd, is going to have any effect, it will be in the closing moments of a tight game. Who knows? Maybe on a borderline foul, as our man battles for a rebound, the official will hesitate for just that one second it takes for the play to swirl past, and after that it's too late.

I've done the same thing on occasion. If we're playing real bad at home, and a call goes against us, I'll prolong my griping or make some gesture of disgust, as of the throwing up of my hands, just to get the crowd hopped up a little bit—on the chance that their emotion will be contagious and the team will get hopped up too.

Everybody does it to a greater or lesser degree. The three Syracuse coaches of my time—Al Cervi, Paul Seymour and Alex Hannum—played upon the home crowd like virtuosos. All three were from the old school of gymnasium ball where every game was a pitched battle. They'd work the crowd up all through the game and, at exactly the right moment, they'd leap off the bench and storm at the officials until you could feel the crowd was ready to march. Of course, they had superior material to work with. Syracuse had a jolly little group of hooligans who, I'm sure, used to call each other up before every game to ask, "Are you going to the riot tonight?"

But Auerbach's temper was no act. It is true that his outbursts may have been timed somewhat more carefully at home, and were quite possibly somewhat louder and longer than was absolutely necessary. Still, they had to be genuine for the most part, because Arnold also blew his top at the officials when we were on the road, where it had to be spontaneous combustion, since he was now getting the wrong crowd worked up against the wrong team. The more the crowd gives it to Red on the road, the more they hop their own team up and the more pressure is being put on the officials against us.

Red has a violent temper. Maybe half-a-dozen times I've seen him become so uncontrollable that he had to be restrained. And every one of these times the man he had to be restrained against was Sid Borgia. Through the years, Arnold and Sid have developed such a fine and genuine and spirited dislike for each other, that they are now poised for battle the second they sight each other on the horizon.

To be an official in the NBA, you have to be a philosopher about such petty things as man's inhumanity to man. All officials know very well what the coaches are trying to do, and Sid, as the senior official, takes these things pretty much in stride . . . except where Auerbach is concerned. As soon as Borgia sees Arnold leap off the bench, he remembers every other fight they have ever had and he has not the slightest doubt that Red's well-turned insults are more personal than strategic. And any time Red feels a call has gone against him, he is sure that Borgia is retaliating against him personally.

Red's famous routine is to jump off the bench screaming, and then throw a little tantrum wherein he stomps his feet in the manner of a war dance. It's a most effective way of calling attention to his complaint because while he could yell his lungs out most of the time without ever being heard above the roar of the crowd, those vibrating boards can be heard all over the arena.

As soon as Red jumps up, Sid comes running over, pointing his finger at him angrily and screaming, "Don't stomp! Don't stomp! It's a technical foul the second you start stomping!"

Early this season, they went for each other as we were leaving the floor in Cincinnati at halftime. While they were being held off, they were screaming insults that went beyond the usual obscenities and into each other's personal lives.

I'm very friendly with Sid, too, and after Red had been pulled into the locker room, Sid said, "Tell Auerbach I shouldn't have made those personal remarks but that the rest of it still goes."

I'm sure that if it had been the other way around Red would have said exactly the same thing. It has reached the point where they're both pretty childish about it. In fact, the reason Borgia isn't officiating in the L. A. series is that Arnold has protested that Sid's personal vendetta against him will put us at a disadvantage.

For Arnold, there will be a special gratification at winning it here. Early in the season when the Lakers were unbeatable and we were sputtering, the Los Angeles papers were calling them the uncrowned champions, a title which presumably made us, the crowned champions, some kind of imposters. Well, we were worse than imposters, we were "Boston's old men." By the time the All-Star game came around, Los Angeles, according to indisputable evidence supplied by its own newspapers, had become "the basketball center of the world."

Red rises to that kind of baiting. As luck would have it, the All-Star game was played in Los Angeles this season, and Red was, of course, coaching the East's team. Chick Hearn, the Lakers' broadcaster, was serving as master of ceremonies at the pre-game luncheon, and when Hearn introduced Red, he very deftly inserted the needle. It was perfectly plain that Hearn was trying to use Arnold to whip up a news item, and I had no doubt at all that Red was going to jump right up and bomb him. I just put my head down and groaned. Even after thirteen years, these situations still embarrass me.

I don't want to sound as if I'm criticizing Arnold here. Maybe we need a few more people around who speak their minds, loud and clear. Still, I think you can squelch someone far more effectively with a few subtle jabs than you can by belting him with a sledge hammer.

You can be sure that Arnold came up swinging his sledge hammer.

You can also be sure that Arnold was booed lustily when he made his appearance on the basketball court that night. I suspect, though, that at this stage of the game Arnold enjoys his reputation for free-style candor almost as much as he enjoys his unpopularity in foreign climes.

In the end, Arnold wins all arguments, to his own satisfaction, because in the end, Arnold's teams always win.

The contribution a coach in the NBA makes to his team bears

no resemblance whatsoever to that of a college coach. In college, a coach stresses the fundamentals. He is a teacher. His work is more basic and more repetitive. An NBA coach is getting All-Americans fed to him on an assembly line. His main job is not teaching but maintaining a harmonious relationship among ten players of widely divergent personalities, backgrounds and styles of play. His job is to mold them into a unit.

Every new man who comes to the team has been the biggest wheel in his college setting. All through his life he has been treated with deference and adulation. The coach's first job is to let a little air out of his tires. I don't know what the other teams in our league do, but I do know that Arnold sets out to teach them the joys of being meek and humble.

The rookie gets all the menial jobs. He automatically becomes our errand boy. He runs out for sandwiches and cokes, he carries the basketballs when we're traveling from exhibition to exhibition.

From the stories I have heard, the bully boys of professional football really degrade and humiliate their rookies. The treatment they get from us is not that rough, but it does serve the purpose of letting the rookie know that his press clippings don't mean a thing and that he had better respect his superiors. As Arnold tells him constantly, "You're nothing but a nothing."

Heinsohn's always moaning that he's the perpetual rookie, because it was three years after his arrival before another rookie stuck with us, and we all sort of got into the habit of giving him all the jazz. Russell got an absolute minimum of it. Partly because he didn't join us until the season was underway and partly because he established himself as a player of stature so quickly. When you have a player who is setting attendance records all around the league, you tend to think twice before you send him down to the corner for a coke.

Because we have always operated off the fast break, Red is primarily concerned with players who can run and—with the exception of Loscutoff, who serves a special purpose—with big men who are well coordinated. The new man has to fit into the Celtics' style of play; we aren't going to adjust our style to suit him.

Given the choice between two players in the draft, Red will always go for the one who has been playing on a winning team, which is as good a key as you can find to his psychology. He feels that if you have been with a loser long enough you begin to think like a loser and you'll be ready to quit a lot sooner under pressure.

Believe me, when you are playing a competitive sport you can tell when a team feels it is going to lose. All of a sudden we'll all be whispering to each other. "Now's the time. Let's break this thing open."

The players who are used to winning, who have the winning spirit, who *expect* to win, will hang in there, battle harder when the tide is going against them, wait for the breaks and either end up winning or come awfully close.

Once the season gets under way, Red's job becomes primarily a matter of off-the-cuff thinking and off-the-hip strategy. A college coach studies the scouting report on the team he is about to play and develops a specific strategy for the specific team. In our league, we know what each team uses and what each player can do. For the most part, it's a question of matching-up the players to the greatest possible advantage to your own side, which usually comes down to a matter of comparative heights. Beyond that, his problem is to make adjustments in his strategy, while the game is in progress, which is roughly comparable to changing horses in midstream at full gallop.

Above all, Arnold is always searching for the little things that can give you that extra little advantage that can make such a difference in a league where everybody is so evenly matched. Back in 1952-53, for instance, we had Ed Macauley, who was a great scorer but a poor jumper. Ed's substitute was Gene Conley, who couldn't score much but could jump through the roof. At the beginning of each quarter, Red would send Gene in for Macauley, just for the tap ball, and Gene would get the ball for us four times out of four.

Well, you should have heard the other coaches scoff at *that*. As they saw it, Red was sacrificing his best scorer for perhaps 1 or 2 minutes (since Macauley couldn't get back until the ball fell dead), for the relatively minor advantage of gaining possession of the ball one time.

Arnold was not really outsmarting himself, though; he figures percentages to the *nth* degree. In pro basketball, the players hit 40 percent of their shots. By getting the ball for us four times out of four instead of having the other team get it, say three times out of four, Red was not only getting us three extra shots, potentially, over the course of the game, he was also taking three shots away from them. Six shots translates, over the long run, to two or three baskets, and two or three baskets can decide an awful lot of games. By the end of the season, every other coach who was equipped to play it the same way had copied it.

I always wore a T-shirt under my jersey in college as a sort of good-luck charm, and I continued to wear it with the Celtics. I wore it, that is, until Arnold blew his top and ordered me to throw it away. His thinking was that the T-shirt would absorb just enough sweat to hang an extra burden of weight across my body late in the game. I'm still inclined to doubt that it would have made the slightest difference, but it does illustrate Arnold's eye for the seemingly insignificant detail.

From everything I have observed, he also makes a great effort to study the temperament of each player. Ramsey being a responsible, dependable, reliable guy is left pretty much on his own. Heinsohn, on the other hand, is good-natured and a little lazy, and so Arnold is always pushing and prodding him. Every once in a while, Tommy will flare back at him with, "Oh, this is Hate Heinsohn Week again, huh?" and they will end up having a heart-to-heart talk. Red will listen patiently to all of Tommy's complaints, agree that perhaps it is time to stop treating him like the perpetual rookie, and it may be all of two days before he is on his back again.

With Loscutoff, he just never lets up. Lusky is his heavy-duty man, and he keeps the needle in him all the time. If Red had his way, Lusky would be in a state of constant anger.

Back in the early days, Arnold used to keep the needle in me too, not directly but in print. But that, I think, was as much to rile the Boston newspapermen as it was to inspire me to greater and more wonderful deeds. Red could see from the beginning that I needed no external pressures to work myself up.

It is common enough knowledge that Red's first allusion to me was hardly calculated to get himself elected president of the local chapter of the Bob Cousy Fan Club. Red was hired to coach the Celtics at the same time I was being graduated from college. Holy Cross had been playing at the Boston Garden during my entire four-year tenure and I had won a certain following as the leading man of what was popularly known as the Fancy Pants A. C.

Since I was a local hot-shot, the Celtics could have had me for the asking. All they had to do was make me their territorial choice.

The Boston writers and the Boston fans seemed to think there was no question that they would take me. I had just become engaged and was making plans to settle down in Worcester, and I hoped and—to be honest—rather felt that they would take me.

But the Celtics, having finished dead last in the league, had the No. 1 draft choice anyway, which meant they had their choice of any player in the country. They were desperately in need of a big man and, as it happened, there was a big, strong 7-footer, Charlie Share from Bowling Green, in the same graduating class. In addition to his extra 11 inches, Share had every bit as strong a college reputation as I did.

In the course of the press conference in which he was being introduced to the Boston writers, Arnold expressed his intention of drafting Share. Immediatey, he was asked how he could possibly pass over the well-known wizard, the Magician of the Hardcourt, Bob Cousy. With that tact for which he is so famous, Red turned to Walter Brown, the Celtics' owner, and snapped, "Am I supposed to win or am I supposed to worry about the local yokels?"

Well, that's Red. Push him just a little and he'll come back swinging.

Now, actually, he was right. The Celtics had already paid out pretty good sums for three of my Holy Cross teammates, George Kaftan, Joe Mullaney and Dermie O'Connell, and they had all sunk without a trace. And Kaftan, for one, had a much stronger reputation than I did. They had tried a couple of Harvard men, Wyndol Gray and Saul Mariaschin, and a Yale man, Tony Lavelli. None of them had panned out either. Neither Red nor Walter Brown had any particular reason to think it would be any different with me and, with a chance to get Share, they had no particular reason to experiment.

If it had been me, I would have made exactly the same decision. When you need a big man and you have a chance to get him, there's no other choice you can make. To get right down to it, there is little doubt that 5 minutes after the Celtics drafted Share they could have traded him for me, plus two other guys and a bushelful of money. Besides, it's human nature to protect yourself when you're choosing your players. I know very well that right now, if I have the choice of giving a scholarship to a 6'7" boy or a tricky little playmaker, I'll take the big guy every time. If I gamble with the little man and he doesn't work out, I can really be second-guessed. No matter how bad the big guy may turn out, I can always say, "Well, at least I went with the percentages."

But the Boston writers had watched me play for years. They had written reams of copy about me, and we had always got along famously. They did not take kindly to an outsider coming in and not only downgrading my ability, and their own assessment of my ability, but doing it in fairly insulting language. Red's talent for public relations is limited.

From what I have heard since, I was the No. 2 man on the Celtics' list, but they never did get a crack at me. Ben Kerner, who was about to operate out of something called Tri-Cities, had seen me play against the Globetrotters and he took me as his No. 1 choice.

Share never did play for the Celtics, and I never did play for Kerner. The story gets almost hopelessly confusing here but, once and for all, let's try to straighten it out.

The NBA had been an unwieldly and generally unprofitable amalgamation consisting of seventeen teams, split up into three leagues. At the end of the previous season, three of the teams had been dropped in a general reorganization, and shortly there-after two other teams, St. Louis and Anderson, folded. (It was in the distribution of the St. Louis players that the Celtics picked up Ed Macauley.)

Doxie Moore, the referee, then took four of the orphaned cities and organized them into something he called the National League. This rump league, quite naturally, set out to sign as many of the NBA players as they could. Jack Smiley, one of the old Illinois Whiz Kids, was hired to coach the Waterloo team and he got ten local businessmen to put up $1,000 apiece to sign Charlie Share. Without giving Walter Brown a chance to meet the price—as Walter would certainly have done—Share signed.

The NBA very quickly moved to protect itself by sending around word that any of its clubs would be permitted to sign a player from any other NBA team if that were the only way to keep that player out of the new league. Ben Kerner immediately got a chance to sign Frankie Brian, a little backcourtman who had been the third-highest scorer in the NBA the previous year. Brian had played for the original Anderson team (which, you will re-member, had folded) and he had been picked up by the Chicago Stags in the same draft in which the Celtics got Macauley.

Brian didn't want to play for the Stags, though. He did want to play for Kerner. He was close to Ben for a reason you could not possibly guess. Kerner had owned the program concession at the Anderson arena, and Frankie had been working for him as an advertising salesman. (Look, this may not be the most fascinating information you have ever heard, but if Frankie hadn't been moonlighting I would have never ended up with the Celtics.)

The Chicago franchise was in financial trouble itself, and it folded soon afterward. Their players were put into another of those draft pools to be distributed around the league. Under these new circumstances, Kerner was given the choice of putting either Brian or his No. 1 draft choice back onto the Chicago roster. And you know who his No. 1 draft choice was. Well, this gave Kerner the choice of an experienced, high-scoring small man or the Magician of the Hardcourt, and he did what any sensible man would do, he kept the known quantity. To this point, my professional career consists of two different teams deciding to take somebody else instead of me. Kerner eventually moved from Tri-Cities, which proved to consist of three small towns clustered at the corner where Iowa and Illinois come together, to Milwaukee and finally, to St. Louis. If it had not been for the rump league, I'd have probably played out my career as a teammate of Bob Pettit.

Kerner traded me to Chicago for Brian in a purely paper transaction. I didn't know a thing about it, though, because the meeting was held in secret at New York's Park-Sheraton hotel. All the owners were informed that I was replacing Brian on the Chicago list, though, and so when Walter Brown went to New York he knew I was available.

Then came the draft. It is always written that only three players were involved, Max Zaslofsky, Andy Phillip and myself. Not true. The entire Chicago roster was being distributed.

The big man on the roster was Max Zaslofsky, an All-Star choice through the entire four-year history of the league. The Celtics assumed they would have the No. 1 choice, since they'd had it in all of the other player drafts. Auerbach gave Brown instructions to pick Max.

The meeting took a different form, however. Valuations had been placed on all the players, to help pay off the Chicago club's debts, but instead of following the regular draft order, the play-

135

ers were assigned to the clubs which could best use them. Everything went along quite smoothly until only the three top-priced players, all backcourtmen, were left. They were Zaslofsky, who was valued at $15,000, Andy Phillip, $10,000 and Cousy, $8,500.

Zaslofsky's name was brought up first, and Brown confidently asserted his priority. Immediately, he was challenged by both Ned Irish of the Knicks and Eddie Gottlieb of the Warriors. They had both been sitting there patiently waiting to grab Max too. Irish insisted that Zaslofsky belonged to the Knicks because Max had been born in New York, educated in New York and would appeal to the Jewish population of the city, an *ex post facto* assertion of territorial rights that might have had far greater validity if Max had not been playing in Chicago for four years.

Gottlieb's claim to Zaslofsky was even more remarkable. Abe Saperstein of the Globetrotters, who had always been very close to Gottlieb, had a phantom deal to take over the Chicago franchise. In anticipation of that happy day—which unfortunately never did come to fruition—Saperstein, according to Gottlieb, had traded Zaslofsky to the Warriors for, of all people, Joe Fulks— which would have been a landmark deal in American sports since it would have broken the Globetrotters' color line.

The argument raged on into the night, with all the other owners becoming increasingly bored. Finally, at about 10:30, Maurice Podoloff, the league president, slammed the table and said, "I'm sick and tired of all this. There's three of you and three players, all backcourtmen. I'm going to put their names in a hat, and whoever you draw, that's who you get."

Podoloff wrote out the names on three slips of paper and put them into a hat belonging to Danny Biasone, the Syracuse owner. "I have never told this to Auerbach," Brown told me once, "because I was ashamed of it. I'm still dead last from the previous season, remember, and I had just been euchered out of Zaslofsky. At the very least, I still had the first pick out of the hat. But I decided to be a gentleman, and I said, 'Ned, I had the first draw in the other two drafts, you can draw first now.'

"As soon as I said it, I could have cut off my tongue. It was the stupidest thing I ever did, because I was giving Irish a 2-1 shot at Zaslofsky."

Irish put his hand into the hat and came out with Zaslofsky. With Phillip and me left, Walter now wanted the experienced

Phillip, who was considered, along with Bob Davies, to be the top playmaker in the league. Instead he came out with me. Walter left the meeting, as he is frank to admit, a tired, angry and beaten man. "I figured," he says, "I'd gotten the dirty end of the stick all around."

Since only one name was left, Gottlieb didn't even bother to draw. He was left with Andy Phillip. All Phillip did was feed Fulks and Arizin so well that the Warriors won the Eastern Division title. Andy led the league in assists for two straight years. Zaslofsky, an individualist, didn't fit into the Knicks' give-and-go attack at all, and he was never a top scorer again.

The Celtics were stuck with me.

As I say, I had not the slightest idea any of this was going on. Having signed to play for Tri-Cities, I had the naïve impression that Tri-Cities was where I was going.

I had been staying with some friends in Worcester, while Missie was fixing up the apartment we were going to live in after we were married, but I had left to drive to New York to visit my folks. My plans were to drive back to Worcester the next morning, pack all my stuff and then start driving toward Tri-Cities. At midnight, Walter reached me at my mother's house, and told me to report to Boston the following morning.

I let out a happy yell. "Mr. Brown," I said, "that's just where I've wanted to play all along."

An interesting footnote to all that intrigue is that the Celtics got Bill Sharman the following year as a consolation prize to that decision to draft Charlie Share. The Waterloo franchise began to founder almost immediately (I will resist any temptation to bring the Duke of Wellington into this), but they somehow got Fred Zollner of the Ft. Wayne Pistons to buy Share for $40,000. The only trouble with the deal was that Zollner had paid the money to the wrong man. As soon as Share stepped over into NBA territory, he belonged to the Celtics. Since we were still desperate for a big, strong man, Brown protested to league headquarters, and Podoloff told Zollner he'd have to come to some kind of accommodation with Boston.

Auerbach, being a great humanitarian, is always willing to extend a helping hand. All he asked for was Bob Harris, who had been Ft. Wayne's No. 1 draft choice that year, plus Bob Brannum, plus Ft. Wayne's No. 1 draft choice the following year. Fortunately for us, the owners—who were still writing the rules as they went along—decided it would not be in the best interests of the league to permit draft rights to be traded away. In place of the draft choice, Auerbach asked for Sharman, whom Ft. Wayne had picked up in another one of those draft pools after the Washington franchise folded.

So the Celtics wanted Share and Zaslofsky, and ended up with Sharman and me. "We picked Cousy's name out of a hat," Walter Brown says, "and we got Sharman as an afterthought."

The stories that there was originally a bit of friction between Auerbach and me over my unorthodox passing is a lot of garbage. Arnold happens to be a very easy coach to play for because he has no rigid preconceptions about how the game should be played. Arnold is the most practical of men. As far as he is concerned, there is only one criterion: "Does the ball end up in the hole?"

The only time he ever questioned any of my moves was at the beginning of my first year. I have always liked to throw the pass the defense isn't expecting. If you are playing defense, for instance, and your man goes past you on a crisscross pattern without getting the ball, you will have a normal tendency to relax. The assumption is that your man is now out of the play. Since he is going for the basket, and you have slowed down, he immediately has a step on you. And that is precisely the point at which I like to hit him with a lob pass.

The only trouble was that my own man was also assuming he was out of the play and he was relaxing too. For the first month or two, I was hitting an awful lot of very relaxed teammates on the head. But that wasn't an unorthodox *pass*, it was an unorthodox *play*.

Arnold kept insisting that there was very little sense in fooling the opposition if I was also fooling my own man, a position that is not without logic. But he also took the position that since the receivers were highly coordinated, well-conditioned athletes, it stood to reason that 90 percent of the time one of my passes was either unexpected or dropped, it had to be my fault.

I felt just as strongly that it was their responsibility to be ready to receive a pass any time they broke into the open. Obviously, though, this was nothing more than a case of their getting acclimated to me, and my getting acclimated to them. By the end

138

of the year, there was no difficulty at all.

After you have worked with a team for any length of time, you know exactly what every man can do. People always seemed amazed that I could flip the ball over my head to Bill Sharman without so much as a glance toward him. "How do you always hit that guy?" they'd ask. "You must have eyes in the back of your head."

Well, heck, that was no problem at all. If, for instance, our 3-on-2 break was stopped, I'd usually swing across to one side to clear out the middle and just drop a pass back over my shoulder, because I knew that Willie would always be following up as a trailer so that he could slip behind me, at the last second for his short jumper.

I do have what seems to be unusual peripheral vision. I can sit in a chair, look straight ahead and see most of the wall behind me. Not with full clarity, perhaps, but well enough so that I can tell what color it is. And that's all you have to catch on a basketball floor, the color of the jersey. So knowing Willie's habits, all I had to catch was the flash of a green jersey behind me. It looks tricky up in the stands, difficult and mysterious. But it isn't tricky, difficult or mysterious. If you put a little lob on the pass, it doesn't even have to be perfect. With Willie's good hands, he's going to get it if it's anywhere near him.

You get to know your teammates so well that you even know how they're going to be moving down the floor on the fast break. I can always tell you who my wingmen are going to be—I don't consciously think about it, I just *know*—and by the time I get down to penetrating territory I know which one I'm going to work with.

Look, if I bust out as quick as I can on the fast break, and I have Sam Jones filling one lane and Loscutoff the other, I know that by the time I'm in position to make my pass, Sam should have almost caught up to me, while Lusky will still be behind. And I also know I'd much rather give it to Sam because of his far superior shooting ability.

But if Heinsohn is coming up as a trailer, I'm aware that he is going to be alert for anything I might do and that with his great hands he is going to hold onto any kind of pass I throw. Rather than pass to either of the wingmen, the percentage is to clear out the middle for Tommy and work for the 3-point play instead of just the basket. Here's how it works:

If I'm working with Sam, and I still have my dribble as I hit penetrating territory (which is the point where my man has to make up his mind either come to me or concede me the chance of going in for a layup), I will cut over toward Sam just enough to give Heinsohn his opening through the middle. When I feel he's busting through there at full speed, I'll turn around and shuffle the ball to him. As I turn, one of the defensemen has got to come dashing across to cover him, but by then—unless I've fouled up the timing—it's too late for him to do anything.

If my timing has been right, he and Tommy will come together at full speed just as Tommy is getting off his shot, which means Heinsohn has got the basket plus the foul. Even if my timing is a little off, Tommy will usually hesitate just long enough to draw the man into him.

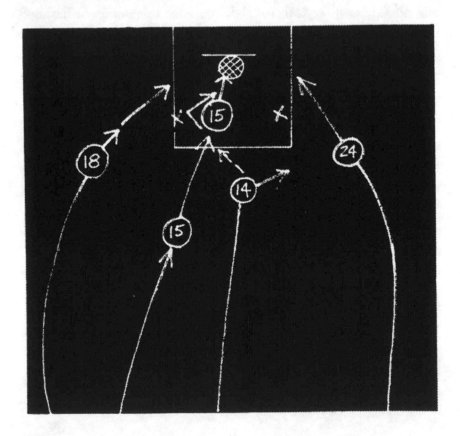

If, on the other hand, my man has come up to meet me as I hit penetrating territory, and I've lost my dribble, I simply pass to Sam and move out myself, drawing my man out of the middle with me, and then Sam kicks the ball to Tommy as he's coming through. Either way, you've cleared out the middle and set up a possible 3-pointer. We can do this because Tommy, Sam and I have become so accustomed to working with each other that we automatically know what each of us is going to do.

We also know what we can't do. I would never throw a behind-the-back pass to Lusky, because he's not always alert to that kind of maneuver, isn't coordinated enough to pick up the rhythm of a developing play and doesn't have Tommy's sure hands.

With Russell, I'd hesitate to use the behind-the-back pass in most situations, but only because he's so tall that I find it difficult to flip the ball up high enough for him. There's no percentage in making a dangerous pass when it's so much easier to throw him an orthodox pass up high enough so that nobody else can reach it.

I'll rarely give Sanders a behind-the-back pass either, and I'll give him few blind passes. Satch drops a lot of balls, and I'm not sure whether it's because he doesn't have good hands or because his contact lenses narrow his range of vision. Normally, I try to put the ball out where Satch can get a look at it before I throw it to him.

My personal relationship with Arnold has become very close, partly because I've been his captain for so long and also because we traveled overseas together for the State Department for three straight years. It was on these overseas trips that I somehow, for reasons that are vague, began to call him Arnold. The rest of the players call him Red.

Because of the association that came out of those trips, I'm the only player on the team Arnold socializes with, even to the extent of going out to a restaurant. In all the years I've been with the Celtics, I have never known him to as much as accept an invitation to spend a casual evening at somebody's house with the boys. On the road, he'll occasionally go to a show with the boys. He'll sit in on a card game on the plane. But that's as far as it goes.

It is a practice with which I thoroughly agree. A basketball team, as I have said, is made up of a very small group of men

141

traveling together and living together. If the coach were to become a part of the group, one of the boys, he couldn't possibly maintain the respect and discipline that is essential to the coach-player relationship.

Red spends most of his spare time on the road with Buddy La-Roux, the only nonplayer available. And yet, it's impossible not to have some interaction of personalities when you're thrown together that much and, although Red doesn't like it, we have had our moments of fun with him. In fact, Arnold is so jealous of the dignity of his position that he becomes an irresistible target.

One year, when we were taking our preseason training up in Ellsworth, Maine, a small town near Bangor, Arnold bought himself a bright red fedora. Oh, how he loved that hat. He wore it everywhere he went for about a week, and his pride in it was so obvious that we began to threaten that we were going to snatch it off his head. Well, that alone was an affront to his dignity. Oh, he'd become livid. "I don't want anyone to touch this hat," he'd say. "Stay away from it, understand! That's an order."

Finally, Macauley and I took up a collection to buy another red fedora from the same store and, as we were reporting to the gym, we placed it on the seat of his car.

After practice, we placed a guy on the locker-room door to let us know when Red was coming. As soon as we got the sign, I ran into the shower. Somebody else grabbed the hat as Red walked through the door. When Red leaped at him to grab it back, the guy threw it to me in the shower. I pulled it down over my ears and just stood there under the shower letting it get soaking wet. Boy, I thought Red was going to die. To really appreciate the story, you not only had to know Red but you had to be there to see the look of utter disbelief on his face. He couldn't believe we would dare do this to him.

As soon as he recovered, he began to scream and stomp and threaten. Right in the middle of his tirade, Macauley came into the shower with a pair of scissors and proceeded to cut various shapes and designs out of the top of the hat.

Arnold went purple with rage. Rather than stand there and be subjected to such rank insubordination and humiliation, he went stalking out to his car. Of course as soon as he saw the other red fedora sitting there, he realized what was going on.

That was a bad year for Arnold, because we pulled another gag on him that I thought was hilarious—even if he didn't. Red is a fast and furious driver. Whenever we have to go anywhere, he'll start about an hour behind us so that he can have the pleasure of roaring past us on the road, smiling smugly. One day we were driving up to Houlton, Maine, to play an exhibition, and Red, as always, found something to delay his departure. Well, that's uninhabited country up there. We just kept driving along a long, straight road for what seemed to be hours without seeing another car, and while we were commenting on it, someone said, "Yeah, but it's just about time for Red to go shooting by."

Things must have been going very well, because we decided to have some fun with him. We pulled off to the side of the road, and just as we were scrambling out of the car, sure enough, there in the distance, shooting toward us, came Arnold's car. We ran out onto the road, flagged him down and told him we'd run out of gas.

"You idiots!" he screamed. "You blankety-blank so-and-so idiots! How can five guys be dumb enough to run out of gas in the middle of Maine? You knew you were going to make a long trip, didn't you? Doesn't even one of you have the elementary common sense to check your gas before you start?"

"Well," we said, looking suitably ashamed of ourselves. "You got to do something. You can't just leave us here."

"That's just what I ought to do, you dumb so-and-sos," he said. "I ought to leave you here to rot. But, all right. I guess I'll have to drive up the road and find a gas station."

As soon as he was out of sight, we piled back into the car and took off. And it couldn't have worked out more perfectly. As we went shooting by the gas station at about 60 mph, there was Arnold, leaning over the gas can with this little old gas man. We just blew the horn, waved and kept right on going, and we were in hysterics for the rest of the way—because, again, you have to know Arnold to appreciate how it kills him to be caught in that kind of a situation, especially by his players. Every time we'd think of his embarrassment at having to go in and explain why he needed a little can of gas, and then his total embarrassment at having to tell the guy he didn't need any gas, after all, we'd go into hysterics all over again.

He passed us on the road again, of course, staring straight ahead. When we finally got to the gym, he didn't say a word to us about it. Not then or ever. As far as he was concerned we couldn't do that kind of thing to him, and so he took the attitude that it had never happened.

Red had his little revenge on me, even though it wasn't necessarily planned. The overseas trips came about because Arnold lives in Washington during the off-season and has a close friend in the State Department. When we were going to France, Arnold assured his friend that no translator was needed. "Cousy," he said with that characteristic confidence, "is a finished linguist." I was finished, all right. I hadn't spoken French for twelve years.

Conversational French came back to me after only a few false starts with the members of the French national team, but basketball French was something else again. Since Red spoke no French at all, I had to first translate their questions from French to English, and then translate his answer back into French. Well, the French words for dribble, backboard, book shots, et cetera, hardly sprung to my lips. My nerves got so jumpy at one point that I couldn't for the life of me think of the French word for ball—which happens to be *balle*.

There were other embarrassing moments, too, even though they become funny in retrospect. In those days, the European and African teams played the game with soccer balls, which is a pretty good trick in that a soccer ball is heavy at the seams, not completely round and generally unbalanced. To give myself a fighting chance, I'd send two basketballs ahead of me to use when I was giving instructions, and then leave them behind for the local kids. When we arrived at Dakar, our first stop in Africa, the balls hadn't arrived. To complicate things further, there wasn't an indoor gym in the whole city, and I had to lecture and demonstrate on a windy day on a court that has been set up alongside the ocean.

My arrival had been well advertised, with the customary superlatives about the "Magician of the Courts" and "the Greatest Basketball Player in the World."

Speaking conservatively, I must have missed the first fifty-five shots. It got so bad for a while that I doubt if I could have thrown the ball into the ocean. I could hear the people muttering to each other. At first they were embarrassed for me and then they were bored with me, and finally they began to wonder, I suppose,

144

whether I might not be some kind of comedian, pulling an international gag on them.

Bill Russell, having thrown up his guts, has rejoined us to catch the end of Auerbach's pre-game talk.

"OK," Arnold says at the end. "This is for all the marbles."

We clasp hands, another timeless ritual, bark out the customary words of encouragement and jog out to the court to join the Lakers.

The Sports Arena is, of course, jammed to capacity, and while we are not greeted by anything remotely resembling a standing ovation, there is, at least, the anticipatory rise of sound. The spectators are happy the game is finally going to get under way.

This is a partisan crowd, especially under these circumstances, but it is not as partisan as in the smaller cities, where a basketball game is viewed as a holy war between their neighborhood and the outside world. Los Angeles is hardly like New York, which has so many transplants that you are almost playing in a neutral city. Still, a Los Angeles crowd is salted with enough people who were brought up in Boston, or at least in the East, so that it does not become violently partisan.

Besides, the team hasn't been here long enough to have really developed the permanent party of hard-core regulars who come to every game and associate themselves completely with the home team. Although, now that I think of it, they've been getting into the swing of things these past two years, especially during the playoff games.

I remember the first playoff game here last year when we had a one-point lead with only seconds to go and thought we had the game tucked away. And then, jeez, Sam threw me a pass from out of bounds, and Jerry West dove in, stole it at half-court, took two dribbles, and let the thing fly. And darned if he didn't make it, just before the buzzer went off. I tell you, it wasn't a roar that went up from the crowd, it was an explosion. I never heard anything like it in my life.

When West was introduced the next night, the cheers were deafening. For that matter, they were deafening for Baylor too. No doubt about it, this is a fantastic franchise Bob Short has here. He has the highest seating capacity—around 15,500—and the highest prices—even higher than in New York. It's a beautiful new arena too, with cushion seats, and not a pole in the place to block the spectators' view.

Los Angeles being Los Angeles, they also have the glamour, led by the resident blond distraction, Doris Day. Miss Day always sits in the front row, just across from our bench, and it is difficult not to watch her and make appropriate comments, not only because we are just as susceptible to glamour queens as anyone else, but also because both her enthusiasm and her appetite seem to be inexhaustible. She will sit there drinking pop and eating popcorn from beginning to end, pausing only to jump to her feet and cheer and shout and shake her fist like the most fanatic of fans.

I cannot but help sneak a look to see if Doris Day is there, because I have a feeling that if she doesn't show up, they're going to call off the game. She's there, all right, in her customary seat and her customary glory, but tonight she's overpowered by Pat Boone, who is there in living color—red pants and yellow shirt.

I dribble the ball a couple of times and shoot. It feels good. Thank the Lord, I feel good. I feel loose. You can't always tell in practice; you can never really be sure until you get into competition. And yet, it is an indication. In that last one in Boston, I had felt just as flat and tired in practice as in the game.

As I get into line to take some layups, I hear my name being called from the sideline. I pay no attention because I'm here to play ball, not to pass the time of day. You can't turn to look at someone and then ignore him. If you nod, you have to say hello; and if you say hello and he indicates he wants to talk to you, you have to go over and reminisce about the good old days. It annoys me to see players on any team fooling around and laughing during a layup drill. And I burn when I see them go off to the side of the court to socialize. *Jeez, you're out here to do a job.* This is what feeds your family, you idiot. This is what you *do.*

In all my years as a professional, I have yet to acknowledge any kind of a call—from friend or from foe. I operate on the assumption that my friends know me well enough to understand, and that the others are only indulging in a childish kind of name-dropping. They're trying to get you to wave or to come over so that they can impress their friends. Big deal.

Maybe I do exaggerate the importance of focusing my concentration entirely upon the game, but I don't know of any other way to generate the enthusiasm I know I need. Early in the year, we were playing an exhibition game in White Plains, New York. As the second half was about to begin, we were all gathered around Arnold trying to hear his instructions while about 1,800 kids were yelling right behind us. Just before we were taking the floor, some guy grabbed my shoulder, and shouted, "Who the hell do you think you are not saying hello to my son. He's been going to your camp for six years." Oh boy . . . I spun around, just furious, and the man scooted away, which made me even more furious because he wasn't even giving me a chance to blast him back.

It burned me so much, just thinking about it, that I sat down and wrote him a scalding letter. I wrote him that I didn't know how he conducted his business but that whenever I stepped on the court, whether it was a playoff game or an exhibition, I was there to play basketball. I sign autographs before the game, I told him. I sign autographs after the game. I sign autographs all week

long. "I'm sure that if you talk this over with your son," I wrote, "he'll understand much better than you seem to."

All right, so I get childish about it. But I guess he did understand, because the boy has already sent in his application to return to camp.

You'd have to be off your head, of course, to acknowledge the hecklers. That's just what they want. The greatest satisfaction

they can get is for the target of their abuse to pick them out. When you don't pay any attention to them, they assume you can't hear them and that makes them scream even louder. And that's the only satisfaction *you* can get. It's the only way you can feel, in a foolish sort of way, that you're getting back at them. *Yell your lungs out, you dirty so-and-so.*

As I go back to the end of the line, I can hear another guy calling to me from the floor. Out of the side of my eye, I see it's some guy in a dark suit, standing right behind the scorer's table.

As I run back after my next layup, Arnold comes over, grabs me by the arm and says, "Come on over here for a second."

He takes me to the side of the court and I see that the guy in the dark suit is Tony Martin. I say hello.

Now, I assume that Martin has asked Arnold to bring me over, and since Arnold knows him pretty well, there probably wasn't much else he could do. But it annoys me anyway, because while the last thing I'd want to do would be to criticize Arnold, he *knows* how I feel about this. We have spent evenings talking about the absolute necessity of shutting off every distraction, every external while you're at work. Unless I'm very much mistaken, it was Arnold himself who first spelled it out to me in specific terms in my first year with the Celtics.

Actually, Martin's a nice guy. I had met him a couple of years previously while he was doing summer stock in Massachusetts. My memory is that Missie and I had a drink with him and his wife, Cyd Charisse, at Ken's Steak House in Framingham. I can pinpoint the time exactly because I had just come up with my famous quote—which was actually a misquote—that "society is rotten to the core."

It was a misquotation, I should add, only in that I hadn't actually used that phrase, possibly because I hadn't thought of it. Misquote or not, though, it's a good example of how anybody in the public eye can get into trouble. I had been invited up to Afton, New York to speak at an awards dinner, and while I was at the house of the man who had invited me I was introduced to a local sportswriter who was anxious for me to meet his kids.

Later, in the question period following my talk, someone asked me about the basketball scandal which had just broken. This is a subject on which I have never hesitated to express an opinion. The point I made, briefly, was that while nobody could condone what those kids had done, we did have to recognize that there was such a thing as relative guilt.

I felt very strongly, I said, that society should assume its share of the responsibility, because it had surrounded its children with corruption every day of their lives. Every time they picked up a paper, I said, there was a new scandal for them to read about. I brought up the GE price-fixing case as an example of the morality that was being practiced by mature, respected leaders of the community; I mentioned the political scandals that had just broken in Massachusetts as an example of the complete amorality practiced by our mature civic leaders; I went into the proselytizing practices that were being tacitly condoned by our mature and respected college administrators, the very men who were presumably charged with fostering and preserving the ethical standards of our civilization.

I added that in their own daily lives they had watched their fathers finagle on their income tax reports and brag about their other small triumphs of cheating and fixing and rampant self-interest.

"And now," I said, in substance, "they become of college age and we expect them to draw a precise line between what is right and what is wrong."

What griped me most of all was that two of the kids hadn't accepted the bribes at all. They had been accused only with failing to report the offers to the proper authorities.

How damn hypocritical can you get? Everything they had been taught from childhood told them that you didn't go squealing to the authorities.

My friend, the reporter, wrote it up accurately enough, but the guy on his city desk tacked on the heading: "Cousy says society is rotten to the core." I have to admit that it is a phrase which catches the eye, because it was picked up all over the country. President Kennedy was holding a weekly press conference in those days. That week, he was unable to make it, and Bobby Kennedy, substituting for him, was asked a question in connection with the decline in the physical condition of our youth. In the course of answering, Bobby pointed to what I had said or, at least to what I had been quoted as saying, and indicated that he endorsed my sentiments entirely.

I would never say that basketball players, or any athletes, should be judged on a different scale of values than anyone else. I do say that whatever scale of values he does develop had better come from his own inner resources, because—and I have been finding this out now that it has become necessary for me to try to attract basketball players to Boston College—he is not very likely to learn very much about the eternal verities from his initial contact with the world of college athletics.

What they seem to be running today is an auction. A mediocre high school player of passable ability and reasonable height will get maybe fifty offers. A really good player will get two hundred. When competition gets that tough, the ante goes up and up, and before you know it—human nature being what it is—the goal becomes simply to get the boy you're after, for no other reason than to win the battle.

We have one of the most sought-after players in the country at Boston College, John Austin of Washington. We got him, frankly, only because Red Auerbach had him at camp, was close to him and his family and convinced them that John would be better off putting aside the more material considerations to attend Boston College and play for me. But the competition from other colleges was unbelievable.

The worst part of it all is that they never stop chasing the boy until he is actually enrolled at another college and sitting at a desk. A boy will send a "letter of intent" to one coach stating that he is going to enter his school, and theoretically that is supposed to be binding. But if the boy changes his mind, possibly because someone else has offered him a better deal, nobody seems interested in holding him to his word. To me, this is disgraceful not only from the viewpoint of the coach, who has probably stopped looking for another boy in that position, but for the sake of the boy himself, who is being taught that a man's word is of no importance at all—who is, in fact, being encouraged to break it.

As a newly signed coach, I have been going around talking to other college coaches, and I find that this is the main topic of conversation among them. Everybody decries it, and nobody is willing to do a damn thing about it. The NCAA has a rule that once a boy has sent a letter of intent to one college, he becomes ineligible to play for any other college in that conference. But the NCAA doesn't seem particularly interested in enforcing its rules, either.

I'd like to be able to say this kind of thing is isolated—but it isn't. We always seem to excuse the dishonesties of our society by first laying down a damning indictment and then practically dismissing it by adding that it is, of course, "only the small minority of corrupt men that can be found in all walks of life" who are involved.

From everything I have seen, the only colleges who do not get into the bidding contest are those very big and rich ones who have huge and influential alumni associations who do their dirty work for them.

I know one thing. I have no intention of going that route. I know it, I say, and yet I also find myself wondering whether as time goes on—and the influence of my name in getting boys to come to Boston College dwindles—it isn't human nature to find yourself compromising your own values more and more until finally, step by step, you find yourself doing all the things you've vowed you wouldn't do.

I can see how easy the rationalizations and justifications can creep in. *You have a job to do, don't you? If you're going to compete you have to compete on the terms you find, don't you? I didn't make the world, did I?*

Well, yes. Within reason, you do make the world you live in. "Within reason," you say? Is that when it starts, when you say "within reason"?

It scares me. Maybe it scares me only because I don't need it. I wanted to get into collegiate coaching only because I love the game and I want to work with kids. Very candidly, I could make two or three times as much money devoting the same time to other kinds of work. I don't see why, with these kind of motives, I should allow myself to sacrifice my own standards of value.

Oh, so that's it, is it? You can afford the luxury of having standards.

It scares me.

This is all something very new to me. When I got out of high school, I had only two offers—straight athletic scholarships and nothing more—and looking back I'm thankful that it worked out that way.

I was born and brought up in Yorkville, in the East 80's in New York, and in those days I played no basketball at all. My day was spent playing stickball and stealing from fruitstands and swimming in the East River.

When I was twelve, we moved to St. Albans, and that was

where I first shot a basketball toward a basket and immediately lost interest in any other sport.

St. Albans was a hotbed of basketball. The high school team— Jackson High School—which was coached by Lou Grummond, enjoyed fantastic success. It was the ambition of every kid in my neighborhood to make the team, and we are talking here of the junior varsity, because you had to pass through the JV's before you could even dream of making the varsity. Well, there were 5,000 kids in school, and the first two times I went out for the team I didn't even get a second look. I made the team, finally, only because I had fallen out of a tree when we first moved to St. Albans and broken my right wrist. For the month or so it remained in a cast, I had to play baseball and handball and anything else that came along with my left hand. By the time I began to play basketball, shortly afterward, my left hand was so strong that I'd be shooting almost as much left-handed as right.

Lou Grummond played a very patterned style of basketball. It was such a rigid pattern that you could even call it a zoned offense. Each player had to do his shooting from a specific and limited area, which meant that one of his players—whom he called the No. 1 man—always came across the middle and shot with his left hand. Left-handers being a distinct minority, the No. 1 man was always the most difficult to find.

Halfway through my sophomore year, Grummond saw me playing in the community center, and came to the conclusion that I was a natural left-hander. After the game, he talked to me about filling the No. 1 position on the JV, and even after I told him that I was a right-hander he asked me to come out anyway.

I played for the junior varsity, did quite well, and was all set to play for the first team in my junior year. I couldn't wait for that summer to end. And then came the most crushing blow of my life. In those days, as now, the schools were terribly overcrowded, so much so that we had to sit double in our home rooms; that is, two kids to each seat. When my first report card came out, I found that my home room teacher had flunked me in Citizenship, our school's word for conduct. I had, it seemed, talked to the kid who was sitting practically in my lap.

I couldn't believe it. I was always a shy, well-behaved boy; I had been brought up, really, to be obedient and respectful. I went running to Grummond, fully expecting him to use his influence, but Lou was a strict disciplinarian himself. He was sore at me, not her. I don't think he has forgiven me to this day. I pleaded with my teacher and I pleaded with Lou. Neither of them budged an inch.

That meant I did not begin to play basketball until the last half of my junior year. In my senior year, I had great success, averaging 17 points a game, which was a heck of a lot of points in those days. Good enough, to be immodest, to make me the leading scorer in the New York City area.

There wasn't the great scramble for players among colleges that there is today, though, and there was particularly no scramble for a boy my size.

Since I had received a certain amount of publicity around New York, I suppose I could have gone to one of the city schools if I had made the first move, although none of them made any move toward me. St. John's University, coached by Joe Lapchick, was the powerhouse in those days, and I have a vague recollection of going over to their dinky little gym with a couple of the other boys on the team. I have an even vaguer recollection of meeting Joe Lapchick, and I believe there was some indication that it was barely possible that a scholarship might be available.

The only real offer I did get during the season came from Boston College. Gen. Al McClellan, the coach, was interested enough in me to come to the house and talk to my folks. He had elaborate plans for a gymnasium they were supposed to break ground on that fall, and I can remember him spreading the blueprints all over the kitchen table. (This is a memory I find rather amusing because they finally broke ground about six years ago—twelve years later—and has been in use for only two or three years.)

I had already made up my mind that I wanted to go to a Jesuit school, so Boston College sounded just great. They had me down to the campus, over a three-day weekend, and while I was tremendously impressed with the Gothic architecture, I also discovered that they had no dormitories. That meant I'd have to be rooming with some family, and while I told myself that I wanted the camaraderie of a dormitory, the truth of the matter is that at that stage of my life I was such a shy boy that the thought of living with a strange family petrified me.

It is possible that I'd have ended up at Boston College anyway, having no other choice, if it had not been for Ken Haggerty, a former Jackson High player, who was playing for Holy Cross. With Holy Cross coming into New York to play Kings Point, Ken talked his coach, Doggie Julian, into coming to see me play. Afterwards, I went to see Holy Cross play and Julian invited me to sit on their bench. That was all. No trip to Worcester to inspect the Holy Cross campus, nothing except a straight scholarship offer. I am sure that if Ken hadn't convinced him I'd be worth the gamble, I wouldn't have been offered that.

But, as I say, I'm happy it worked out that way. My father was a taxi driver and we were relatively poor. We were able to own our house in St. Albans only by living in the cellar, sleeping in the attic and renting out both the first and second floors.

In those days, $5.00 was a fortune to me. I suppose most kids today would consider $100 a fortune. So if they offer you a down payment on a car or if they offer to let your sister or your girlfriend go to school, or they buy a house for your folks, it seems as if they are giving you all the money in the world.

By any mature standard, what they offer is nothing. Set against your earning capacity once you have finished college, what's a couple of thousand dollars?

I hear the echo coming back! "Why knock it? What's wrong with giving a poor kid a couple of thousand dollars?"

What's wrong is that the kids are being told, at that impressionable time of their life, that putting a ball in a basket is a skill of such overriding importance that grown and influential men are willing to come groveling at their feet. Having already been put on a pedestal in their own high school world, why shouldn't they believe it. And having been taught by mature, responsible people, the pillars of our society, that there is nothing wrong with making an under-the-table deal to go to college, why shouldn't they be somewhat receptive to an under-the-table deal to shave points. I'm not condoning shaving points. I'm simply getting back to the question of relative guilt. Because it's those same pious businessmen, hustling alumni and eye-closing administrators who are so damn ready to cast the first stone. Well, I think it's fair for these kids, as mitigating evidence, to look the rock-throwers right in the eye and ask the question, "Who taught me?"

Now I am going to talk about something I'm terribly ashamed of, and it will be interesting—in connection with this very point of relative guilt—for you to study your own reactions to it.

A couple of years ago, in the middle of the season, Frank Scott (who is a sort of liaison man between Madison Avenue and athletes) called to tell me he had a cigarette commercial lined up for me. I had always turned down any kind of cigarette endorsements because I believe smoking is very bad for kids. An athlete does have one value. Children, being great imitators, look up to us and we can try to be decent people and provide good examples. There is no man alive who hasn't done many things he is ashamed of, so it becomes a question of being relatively careful.

Frank told me all I had to do was fly to New York in the morning, make the commercial, and I'd be back in Boston by early afternoon. I don't know why the devil I did it—my brain must have been paralyzed or something—but I just automatically flew down, did the commercial and flew back.

The day after the commercial came out, the letters started to come in. Not that many, really, but the first one was enough to make me realize I had made a terrible mistake.

I called Frank immediately to ask him to go back to the agency and tell them that if they would tear up the contract I would return their fee and reimburse them whatever it had cost them to get the thing on the market.

Naturally, Frank wanted to know what was the matter.

"I just feel strongly about it," I told him. "Other than that, I've been getting letters about it, and it has me upset. I don't think we've done the right thing here, Frank."

In order to get the agency to take it off, Frank apparently told them I was very upset because I had been getting a great deal of mail on it. Well, that's all they needed. Take it off, my eye! They printed more posters and they flooded the country with fliers. They had them in drugstore windows all over the country and they plastered them all over the New York subway cars. The contract ran for a year, and in that year any kid could learn that Bob Cousy was very high on the therapeutic value of cigarettes.

158

I suggested, at the beginning, that you make your own moral judgment on this kind of thing. I would suspect that a good percentage of you are at a loss to understand what I'm making all the fuss about. It is a sign of accomplishment to be asked to barter your name to endorse a commercial product. It's a prime status symbol: you've made it, Jack! (I am not against advertising and endorsements, understand. I think it's fine to endorse any product you believe in and use, and I've endorsed my share.)

All I had done, after all, was sell my name and my reputation. I don't even remember how much I was paid; maybe a couple of thousand dollars. I had lied. I had encouraged kids to do something I knew could only hurt them—especially if they wanted to be basketball players—and I had done it for money. If that isn't a definition of corruption, I need a new dictionary.

What I did, I think, is every bit as serious as taking $500 to win a game by 10 points instead of 15.

PART FOUR:

THE GAME

I SHAKE HANDS with Tony Martin and resume practicing until the horn sounds to indicate that the game is about to start. As we gather together in front of the bench, I suddenly remember that I want to remind K. C. Jones and Havlicek to stay on Barnett and play him almost a full man to the left. Not that they need to be reminded. I need to know I reminded them, just to clear it out of my mind.

The game starts with Russell jumping against Wiley. The Lakers come up with the ball and it goes to Jerry West. He jumps, misses. Baylor picks up the rebound, shoves it back to LaRusso, and Rudy pops in a two-hand set shot from outside.

Oh, oh, that's all we need. Let's hope that with Tommy boxing him away from the boards so well, LaRusso doesn't come up with a hot hand from outside.

But that's just a vagrant thought. I feel good. I'm up on my toes, the way I should be, not flat-footed the way I was in Boston. It's going to be all right.

I come back up with the ball, running easy, running loose, and bounce a pass to Sam Jones. Sam kicks it back to me, 6 or 8 feet in from the left-hand corner. How did I get over here? I take a

long one-hander, a shot I wouldn't normally take from that position. As soon as the ball leaves my hand I know it's in. As long as the shot is, I barely feel it leave. When you shoot the ball right, it's the same as when you hit a golf ball right. You don't really feel

as if you've hit it, because the clubhead has done all the work. In basketball, the wrist and follow-through should be doing the work. The wrist should be loose. If the wrist is tight, you'll have to strain to get off a long shot like that.

Yes, I feel great. Just the opposite of the Boston game. Instead of the sudden, deflating release of energy, all that pent-up energy is releasing itself slowly and evenly. I feel as young as I did ten years ago. It's going to be all right.

Besides, you pick up confidence by making your first shot.

I call my own number coming down the floor—the 1-play. The play starts out just like Russell's 3-play, with Russ coming up high, and Sanders swinging underneath the basket to clear out the right side, then buttonhooking around so that he's in good rebounding position. On my play, though, I give the ball to Sam Jones and come down on the left-hand side of the court.

Sam kicks the ball in to Russell and follows in behind it, stopping just before he gets to the foul line, a little to Russell's right. I have been continuing down the left-hand side of the court, bringing my man in deeper than the foul line. But as Sam hits his spot, I'm already cutting back and swinging up and around the double-pick he and Russ have set for me. As I swing behind them, Russ gives me the ball.

If my man has tried to fight me all the way around, he's behind me and I simply continue around to the basket, because that whole side has been cleared out. That's the first option on the 1-play. That's the play I'll take if I can get it.

If Russell's man switches to me, Russ goes straight in for the basket and, with my little man on him, I can give him the same high pass I'd give him if he were running the same option on his 3-play. I can also continue my drive around the key because I'm in full stride and I should be able to get a good step on that big a man before he can untangle himself. After all, I only have to drive about 15 feet.

If instead of following me around, my man cuts in front of Russell and Jones to block my drive, I now take advantage of the double-pick and take a 17-foot one-hander. That's my second option.

Selvy does cut in front of the double-pick. I stop, take my one-hander, and it couldn't go in sweeter.

West sinks two quick baskets to put the Lakers ahead, and then LaRusso sinks another long set to put them ahead, 9-5.

Baylor misses, and Sam picks up the ball, feeds me nicely and I drive down the middle looking for the 3-pointer. Selvy belts me good as I'm trying to get the shot away, but I have the two foul shots. I sink them both. The game is tied again.

Selvy drives in close, jumps into me as if he's going to shoot, but at the last split-second he sees Wiley standing free, as Russ moves over to double-team Baylor. But Wiley isn't alert and the ball bounces off his hands and goes out of bounds.

I can see Selvy grimace. He had his shot there, and he gave it up and lost the ball. That can discourage a man. I've been scoring, that can discourage him too. That can keep him from breathing down my throat for the next few seconds. Tommy has been driving in on LaRusso, with and without the ball. Let's give Rudy something to think about too. As I start down the floor, I put up four fingers, the signal for Heinsohn's play. The play really is for me to pass off to Tommy on my left and then clear out to the right side of the court. Heinsohn then dribbles back to the foul line, turns to face the hoop, and either takes his jump shot behind Russell's pick or, if he sees an opening, drives down the middle.

But as I hold up the fingers, I also flip them back toward myself to indicate to Tommy that I want the ball back. Tommy picks the signal up perfectly, dribbles up to the key, gives it back to me, and picks beautifully so that I have only to move a step to my left to put him directly between me and Selvy. Again, I know from the moment the ball leaves my hand that it's good. We're leading, 11-9.

West's shot gets deflected on the other end of the court, and we're down into penetrating territory again. Selvy, who's getting mad now, darts in to try to intercept a pass that's coming to me out of a scramble. He just misses, and whirls around quickly, trying to recover his balance. But I have room to drive right through him. I'm in for a close one-hander, and—damn—I miss.

And wait a minute . . . just wait a minute . . . Wait a darn minute. What am I doing? I'm supposed to be the playmaker on this team, and all I can see is the basket. Simmer down. Everything's going to be all right, just simmer down.

Playmaking is an art, and while there are no hard and fast rules to art, there are disciplines, which amounts to the same thing. The first discipline of playmaking is that you have to *think* of yourself as a playmaker. *You have to think of shooting as an aid to playmaking, not the other way around.*

The rules of playmaking develop out of experience and practice and meditation and are therefore carefully planned—initially. In the end, they must become—like all offensive moves—wholly automatic. You program your mind, much as you would program a computor, and then the machine takes over and runs the show. It is when the playmaker himself throws the computor out of kilter—manmade errors, as we cyberneticists say—that you have to catch yourself, make the necessary adjustments in your mind and set the machine whirring smoothly again.

My own rules may be listed as:

1. Don't pass just to get rid of the ball. Always have a definite purpose in mind.
2. Don't press for opportunities to set up your own shots, but still shoot often enough to keep the defense honest.
3. Keep the other players on the floor happy by giving them their share of scoring opportunities.
4. Reward the players who are hustling.

There are now, as there have been in the past, many excellent backcourtmen. The two I find myself mentioning most often are Dugie Martin and Larry Costello. They don't throw the ball away, they can shoot from outside and they are bears on defense. But they are not what I call playmakers. They are passers.

The playmaker never passes just to get rid of the ball. Every pass is made with a purpose in mind. The purpose is to move the defense in such a way that, speaking generally, the man he passes to is the man who is in position to shoot and, more important still, to take a shot that is a good one for him, percentagewise.

There are not many playmakers around, and they are growing scarcer by the year. The only one who has come around in the last five years or so has been Oscar Robertson. In the old days, Dick McGuire was an excellent playmaker. Andy Phillip was a good one. George Senesky was pretty good too, and maybe Bob Davies. And that's about it.

The playmaker's first job is to move the defense over in such a way that he develops the opportunities for the shooter *before* the pass is made. This is what nobody seems to understand. Tommy Heinsohn, for instance, is always called a "gunner," a word that isn't to be taken as a compliment since the connotation is that once Tommy gets his hands on the ball, all he wants to do is shoot. Well, that's just the way he should feel.

For Heinsohn to get the ball, set a pick for someone else and then pass it back doesn't really make any sense, because if I am doing my job right, Tommy should be confident that any time I give him the ball he is either in position to get his shot away or in position to look for the opportunity to make his play. Once he has this confidence, he is mentally primed to make his move instead of wasting that vital split-second wondering whether or not to make it.

A forward doesn't touch the ball that often over the course of a game, anyway, so if he is going to hit his average, he's got to be looking to make his opportunities and leave the worrying about the other guy's shooting opportunities to me.

Furthermore, Tommy moves very well *when he doesn't have the ball*—cutting, faking and digging—which means he has worked to put himself into the best possible position by the time the ball hits him.

For purposes of illustrating how a playmaker can move the defense, let me start with the most spectacular—and easiest—example: a 3-on-2 situation off the fast break.

I am coming down the middle with my two wingmen spreading out each side of the court. Each of the two defensive men is going to be retreating, holding themselves between me, one of the wingmen and the basket. What the defensive man is doing is fighting a delaying action. He knows the other three defensive men are racing down to cover, and what he should be doing is throwing defensive fakes at me to try to get me to stop my dribble up around the circle, before I enter penetrating territory. He is quite willing, under these circumstances, to concede me a shot from there. What I am trying to do is to get a layup out of it.

My first concern, then, is to penetrate deep enough so that one of the two defensive men has to come and get me or concede me a very close shot. When he makes up his mind to come and get me, I am going to make sure that he commits himself completely, taking him completely out of the play.

Let's say, I have Heinsohn in the left lane and Sanders in the right, and I have decided to work the right side of the court. As I get into penetrating territory, I slant off slightly to the right. If the defensive man between me and Sanders doesn't commit himself totally—if he simply fakes and tries to play it cute or insists on holding his position between us—I have only to take one more step and leap in for a layup.

On the other hand, I have to be careful not to penetrate too deeply before I force him to commit himself. If I do, I have narrowed my working area to too small a zone under the basket, and he will be able to cover me and still turn back, after the pass, and bother Sanders.

When I pull him away from Sanders I want to open up the greatest possible gap under the basket, and I want to time it so that he has no possible way of getting back.

So I slant off to the right, make sure the defensive man has committed himself completely to me, and now the whole area

under the basket has been opened up. As the man comes to me, Sanders breaks for the hoop. I have only to pass off to him, and he, free as a bird, has only to take his one step and he's in under the basket for his layup.

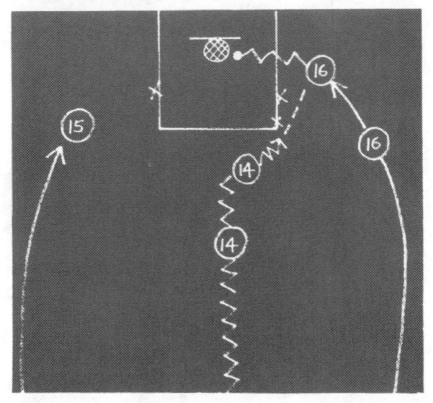

On a balanced situation, 3-on-3, you can move the defensive alignment, under the proper conditions, by "showing the man the ball," another fairly spectacular technique. As I come down the middle and hit penetrating territory now, I have a man covering me and a defensive man on each of my wingmen.

Let's say Ramsey is in the right-hand lane here and I know he is coming fast. I slant sharply out toward the right, bringing my own man with me and moving directly toward the man covering Rams. And now, instead of protecting the ball with my body, I open up my dribble for one second, putting the ball right under his nose. I am deliberately breaking the cardinal rule of basket-

ball, which says that you always protect the ball.

Ramsey's man, seeing that ball suddenly exposed and coming right toward him, finds it almost impossible not to take a swipe at it or, at the very least, to turn his head and look at it. As soon as Rams sees his man take his eyes off him, he seizes his opportunity and cuts for the basket. I pull the ball back, bounce a pass to him, and before the defensive man can recover, Rams is through for the basket.

It isn't that the defensive man doesn't know what I'm doing—a second after it's done. It's just that he's so startled to see the ball in his face that reflex action takes over. The impulse to go for the ball is almost irresistible.

I would never dare do that to a Dugie Martin or a Larry Costello, because their reflexes are so fast and their hands are so quick and they are built so close to the ground that, in that split-second, they'd have an excellent chance of snapping the ball right away from me. But normally, I'm working with a 6'6" forward on that play, and he doesn't react that fast. I'm betting my quickness against his quickness, and I've given myself the added edge that for one split-second I know what I'm going to do and he doesn't.

If he doesn't bite, if he holds his defensive position even after I've put the ball in his face, I will keep coming on until I'm directly in front of him. I am now between him and Ramsey, and I have only to slip the ball back to Rams, and pick for him.

Either way, I have done the most that could possibly be done to develop the play.

You will notice, though, that the defense makes up your mind which way you're going to go.

You cannot predetermine the play as you're coming down the floor. You do everything possible to make the defensive man do what you want him to do, but you still have to wait until he does it. You cannot get stubborn about it and try to force your play if it doesn't fall the right way for you.

You will notice, too, that you are totally dependent upon having good players on the floor with you. You are counting upon your own man, having played hundreds—or even thousands—of games with you, to break when that man turns his head or, if it goes the other way, to react to the developing pick. You are also dependent, in moving the defense, upon having the opposing players react to your moves the way a good player should react.

In order to move the defense, a playmaker has to be a scoring threat himself.

This is especially true on the fast break, where you don't really know what plays are going to materialize until the defense makes them materialize or, putting it another way, *you make them materialize* by manipulating the defense. If the man covering you is confident he can fall off you, either because you are a poor shooter or a reluctant one, it becomes that much more difficult to open up the scoring zone. If, as an example, the defensive man knows you are always looking to pass on the 3-on-2 break, you are not going to get him to commit himself totally. He is going to throw a fake at you, fall back on his own man and break up a certain amount of plays.

It works the other way too. If you are so anxious to force a layup for yourself that you ignore your open man when the defensive man comes to you, you are making things easier for the defense and tougher on yourself. In other words, you cannot become stereotyped. You must, again, take the best opening the defense leaves you.

A playmaker must be a scoring threat, then, in order to move the man covering him over to where he wants him to be. If the defensive man knows I'm not shooting, he can defense me, in effect, much as he would defense a man who could only go to his left. Only in this case, the whole team is affected, not just one man.

Once they know I am not looking to shoot, the defense sags off as I enter the penetrating area, and instead of opening the area up for the other players on the team, I'm choking it off. I've got to shoot enough to draw the defense in to me.

I had to make an adjustment of sorts in my last five years in the NBA. In college, I had been pretty accurate with a running one-hand shot from about 25-30 feet out. Once I got up to the pros, there were so many other things I could do, working with such good players, that it wasn't a percentage shot for me to take and I abandoned it.

As I grew older, though, and a little slower, I recognized that I needed a little more room to maneuver around in. I wanted to be able to start my moves from a little farther out, so that when I faked and went for the basket I wouldn't be moving into a congested area. The obvious thing to do was to reactivate my old

running one-hander. In the first month or so of the season I was hitting like heck with it, and it was serving its purpose nobly. But the defense studies your new moves, too. (That's why some rookies will look great on their first swing around the league and then disappear from sight.)

After a couple of swings around the league, I found that my man would come leaping into me as I was taking that shot and either deflect the ball or bother me enough so that I was losing all accuracy. It took only a little analysis for me to realize what was happening. In taking the shot I had to come off my dribble, go up off my left foot and bring the ball up to my shoulder. My trouble was that as I brought the ball up, I was pausing for about a second before I released it.

Once you give up your dribble, you have to either shoot or pass, which meant my man didn't have to hesitate a moment before rushing in on me.

I continued to use it for the rest of the season, just to show that I had it, but it was a remarkably ineffective shot.

During the summer, at camp, I started to experiment with taking the running one-hander off the wrong foot, even though it violated every principle of shooting. When a right-hander shoots off the left foot, his whole body is flowing through toward the basket in one continuous fluid motion, with the power of the shot coming off the momentum of the body and the follow-through of the arm.

When you shoot off the right foot, you're going against the grain. Your momentum carries you across your body now, and you lose almost all of your follow-through.

On the other hand, having no follow-through, it becomes completely a wrist shot, and a wrist shot is far more accurate. Without getting overtechnical, when the movement of the arm is cut down, the margin of error is cut down along with it.

The only follow-through you do have on a wrist shot comes from the snap of the wrist itself, but I found in working it out in practice, that I was able to get all the additional power I needed by starting the shot at the waist instead of the shoulder, and bringing the ball up in one continuous motion.

The beauty of it was that I could go directly at my man and bring the ball up at the same time I was taking that final dribble off my right foot. You don't give the shot away at all and you

182

completely eliminate that business of having to come up off the left foot and pose.

Unorthodox as the shot was, I found it quite comfortable almost from the beginning. The next year, I put it right into action and I had so much success with it that over the last couple of years at least 75 percent of my outside shooting has been done off my right foot.

Since it was that effective and since I could get it off that quickly, I was able to draw the defense in to me, which was the purpose of it all to start with.

Dick McGuire, for all his immense ability as a playmaker, had only that one weakness. Dick simply refused to shoot although I know very well that his coach, Joe Lapchick, pleaded, cajoled and screamed at him to shoot for six or seven years. New York's give-and-go style was built around Dick's playmaking ability, and he was good enough so that even with the defenses sagging all around him, he could still ram the ball through often enough to be effective. But he was nowhere near as effective as he would have been if he were a scoring threat himself. It wasn't that he couldn't shoot, either; Dick wasn't a bad shooter at all.

Oscar Robertson is exactly the opposite. The thing I like most about Oscar as a playmaker—when he is operating as a playmaker—is that he has no wasted motion. Every pass he makes is made with a purpose.

But Robertson is also one of the game's superscorers, and he is most effective as a scorer when he is working his way in close by maneuvering and bulling his man. But when you're getting into penetrating territory with the ball, you have to be conscious, primarily, of setting up a play. You can't have it both ways. If you are concentrating on maneuvering your own man so that you can get your own shot, you can't also be thinking about moving the defense to set up a shot for anybody else. When Oscar does have to pass off under those circumstances, he is passing out of necessity, he is just getting rid of the ball. At this point, he is no longer really a playmaker. When he wants to, though, Oscar can do everything. He has more basketball sense, as far as moving the defense and then utilizing the correct pass, than anybody who has come into the league in recent history. And on a fast break, he does have the reflexes to enable him to look for his shot and at the same time watch for the developing play.

Oscar has so much talent that an argument could be made that Cincinnati is most effective in having him operate the way he does. I suspect, however, that it is simply bad practice for a playmaker to also be the team's greatest scorer. The two talents are not cumulative; there's a point where the law of diminishing returns sets in.

You must keep the four other players on the floor happy by giving them their share of the scoring opportunities.

Basketball is not a game of solitaire. One great scorer, for instance, does not win games for you, as Wilt Chamberlain has proved. The argument can be made that Chamberlain suffers only from a poor supporting cast. If you have a man who makes better than 50 percent of his shots, the argument goes, why shouldn't you concentrate on getting the ball to him whenever possible. Carrying that to its logical conclusion, I would have to ask why you should ever let any other player on the team shoot at all. No, statistics mean nothing in basketball.

Robertson averages better than 30 points a game, has the best shooting average of any backcourtman in history and also leads the league in assists—which, out of my own prejudices, is the only statistic that means a thing. If he's doing everything better than anybody else, then why shouldn't he be left alone to do them.

The answer is quite simple. On a professional level, basketball is a team game and a two-way game. Given a better shot at the ball, the other players on the Royals—and the Warriors—would play better all-around ball.

By the nature of the game, a playmaker has the ball 75-80 percent of the time. If he is also doing most of the scoring, he is going to have the ball 80-85 percent of the time. You cannot expect everybody else on the team to go all out on defense and continually hustle on offense for the privilege of watching Robertson put on a one-man show. Just as you cannot expect the forwards and guards on the Warriors to battle for the ball on defense so they can give it to Chamberlain and then stand back and watch him shoot. It isn't that they consciously sulk. It's simply that human nature just doesn't work that way. Every man on both those teams was an All-American in college. They all made their reputations as shooters. They want a piece of the ball too.

The Celtics don't have a big scorer; we have balanced scoring. The Celtics don't pay their players according to the statistics. Our salaries are based on our contribution to the team.

I have always tried to balance off the forwards. If I find I've been coming down on the right side of the court too much, I'll shift over and start coming down on the left. Nobody gets overlooked, and the Celtics keep hustling and winning.

Sure we've had players of great ability. But the way the game is played today it's not a question of sheer ability. The team that makes the least mistakes, plays the most intelligent ball and gets the maximum contribution out of all ten men will be the team that wins.

Just being aware that the job of the playmaker is to keep everyone happy builds compound interest for you. Because the very fact that you are aware of it keeps you alert to everything that is happening on the floor.

When I get the ball on an outlet situation, I'll be standing near the sideline, just about even with the foul line. Russell has taken the rebound, he kicks it out to me and as I start to kick in to the middle, I automatically glance out at the floor. With just normal peripheral vision, I see with that quick glance where everybody on the floor is placed.

As I start down the floor, I can project where each of those men is going to be when I hit the penetrating area, and I am therefore going to be ready to make my move before I get there.

If I have, in that quick, encompassing glance, seen Tommy Heinsohn and, let us say, Woodie Saulsberry start together down the left lane, I know that by the time I've reached the foul line, Tommy, as a man who will be running at full speed without the ball, is going to be ahead of him. I can keep looking to the right and at the last moment kick it to the left and Tommy is going to be there.

I've never thought of this before, but I know it's true. Although I'm looking for my own men when I take in the placement of players on the floor, I am also noting the position of the defensive men in relation to them, and automatically programming how the defense is going to be positioned in relation to the offense.

I picked Saulsberry as an example, because he is known around the league as one of those guys who gets lazy away from home. And so if he is guarding Heinsohn or Sanders under the conditions I have posited, I wouldn't have the slightest doubt that either of them is going to beat him down the court, even if they've started out a little behind.

On the other hand, he's pretty fast when he wants to be, so if we were playing on his home court, and Woodie was having a good night, I would automatically discard the blind pass to his man under these same conditions. I'd want to glance over and make sure.

Reward the players who are hustling.

If Russell or any of the forwards goes up and battles under the boards, finally gets the rebound and, instead of putting it up himself, throws the ball out to me because I seem to be in the clear then, free or not, I'll usually kick it right back in to him. Strategically, it's a good play, because normally the man he's been fighting with relaxes. Above and beyond strategy, though, it's a good play psychologically. He's fought like hell, and he deserves the chance for the basket.

I've been standing back there out of the action, doing nothing. If I put up a one-hander and miss, after all his work, he isn't going to be very happy. Even if I shoot and make it, time after time, he isn't going to keep fighting off those boards so I can stand there comfortably and pile up the points.

Off the defensive boards, it's even truer. Let's say one of the big forwards—Sanders, say—gets the defensive rebound and kicks it to me for the fast break. As I take my quick look before I head

down the floor, I see that he's given me the ball and he's digging down behind me as a trailer. Now, there is only one way a trailer play can develop. The offensive man has simply got to make up his mind that he's going to beat the defensive man down the floor through sheer guts, sweat and determination.

All right, here you have a man who has already done his job in getting the rebound and now, in addition, he's sprinting the full length of the floor. I'm going to give him the ball, baby. Sanders is going to get that ball whether he's free or not because, dammit, he's busted his tail and he deserves the shot at the basket. I'm going to forget all about percentage shots now; I don't care if I've got a man hanging under the basket. I'm going to flip the ball back to Sanders.

I don't care that I normally don't want to give Sanders a behind-the-back pass, either. I'll either put it behind my back or I'll give up some of the advantage of the fast break and let him come

up alongside of me. I'm willing to give up the basket if I have to because I'll give up two points any time to make sure we hold on to that kind of spirit and hustle.

The basket is important, sure. But it's far more important that everybody keeps digging.

There's another psychological factor involved here. The center and the forwards have to race up and down the full length of the court. As a guard, I'm playing what amounts to half-court basketball. Satch has run 90 feet, battled under the boards, got the ball and he's now running 90 feet back. I'm going from foul line to foul line, 50 feet up and 50 feet back.

He may battle off that board once and race down the court; he may battle a second time and race down; but if he doesn't get the ball, he isn't going to be battling quite so hard the third time, and you can be darn sure he isn't going to be racing down the court.

I'm not only talking about defense. For everybody except the playmaker, who can get his kicks out of setting up the play, the fun of this game is in the scoring. The rest of it is hard work. Where you set up an offense in which four guys are supposed to work so the other guy can play, you're going to end up with four guys standing around.

To play good offensive basketball, you've *got* to have movement. You've got to have players who will run and cut without the ball. Well, that's hard work too. If they keep cutting and you don't hit them with the ball, they're just not going to move anymore. I've seen it happen a thousand times. I wouldn't do it, and you wouldn't do it. You will not continually wear yourself out, cutting and breaking, if you are not getting the ball.

When Sam Jones came to the Celtics he was the fastest human I'd ever seen on a basketball floor. In college, he used to do it all by himself. Suddenly, he found he was supposed to give the ball over to me and cut for the hole. The only way to convince him under those circumstances that our way was the best way for everybody, was to hit him with the ball when he did what he was supposed to do. He gets the ball, he scores the points and he's happy.

Nine out of ten times that I see a man cutting, I will hit with a pass, or at least try to. It isn't anything we've sat down and discussed. It's something they know from experience. If they do the work, they'll get the ball. Putting it the opposite way, if they *want* the ball, all they have to do is put out that extra effort.

It's the simplest kind of psychology but, again, if you're not aware of it you're not practicing it.

To a degree, it goes against your own human nature. Even though a pretty pass has always given me a greater thrill than a basket, I like to score too. But I have the greatest reward of all. I control life on that court the way it is impossible to control life outside. I have my own little world, a lighted patch, 90 feet by 50 feet. I control the ball, I control my team and, to some extent I control the movements of the opposition. I am the Big Daddy who hands out the rewards and inflicts the punishments. Do a good job and I reward you by giving you the ball. Go for my fake, and I punish you by slipping the ball past you. I have my own external rewards too. When I do a good job I am rewarded by the applause from out of the darkness.

In the complex world outside, life controls you. In that lighted patch, I control life. Reward and punishment, minute by minute. Life is simple inside that lighted patch.

I have not included the behind-the-back stuff in the theory of playmaking, because it falls more under the heading of technique than of basic philosophy. All this behind-the-back garbage has been so exaggerated, anyway, that people seem to think I do it as a matter of routine. If I dribble behind my back eighteen times a season, that's a lot. Ninety percent of my moves have always been completely orthodox. I didn't originate it by a long shot, either; players had been doing it for years.

It came about, originally, purely by accident. Some time back, you will recall, we talked about Barnett's weakness of going exclusively to his left. Well, every player prefers to go in one direction or another, and even though you practice using both hands and varying your movements it is very easy, in the heat of battle, to find yourself, going exclusively to your stronger side. Actually, it isn't you who notices it first. Your opponent notices it, and he picks the most opportune time—for him—to call it to your attention.

In my junior year at Holy Cross we were involved in a very tough game against Loyola at the Boston Garden. With a minute to go, they were leading by 1 point. We had possession of the ball, though, and the play was for me to drive in so that if I didn't get the basket I'd have a good chance of picking up a foul, and probably a two-shotter.

Well, Loyola had pretty much read our plans, and either their coach or the man covering me had apparently noticed that I had been going exclusively to my right all night. With 20 seconds to go, I started driving into the key from the left side of the court. My man stayed right with me and he was now playing me a full man to the right. If I had straightened out at the key and driven right on in, as I had intended to, I would have run right over him. If I tried to swing around him, taking the long route around, I'd have ended up out near the baseline, a very tough shot.

Without thinking at all, I slapped the ball behind my back, dribbled a couple of times with my left hand and, as I changed direction, put up a left-handed shot. It wasn't done with any tremendous ease, because the man still had me closely covered, and I got the shot off rather awkwardly—but it went in.

It isn't really that difficult for anybody and, because of the way I'm built, it isn't at all difficult for me. Auerbach always says you have to be a freak to play this game, and as one of the game's foremost freaks I'm inclined to agree with him. I sometimes think that after Dr. Naismith put up that peach basket in his Springfield gym, he went back to his classroom and drew the blueprint for me. I have abnormally long arms and massive hands, the better to handle a basketball with. I also have heavy legs to absorb the shock of pounding up and down the floor. He'd have given me about 3 more inches if he had been on the ball, but I can't complain too harshly even there. How was he to know that a 6-footer was going to be a midget!

There was one other oversight, too. I am not a fast runner. People always give me that sidelong, aw-come-on look when I say that, but it's quite true. Even in my best days, I was never a fast runner.

I give the illusion that I'm running much faster than I really am because I have fast hands, quick reflexes, and I can start and stop quickly. The point is that a backcourtman doesn't have to be fast. As I have already said, I do not play the full court. I am normally patrolling a fairly restricted area between the top of our key and the top of theirs.

When I'm looking to set up my own play, I'm just above the top of the key. All I have to do is throw a fake at my man, kick into the center, and I have automatically picked up at least a half-step on him. If you use your body correctly, that's all you need. It's now merely a question of getting to the penetrating area as quickly as possible and keeping your body between the man and the ball. In the 22 feet I have to cover, a man of normal speed simply hasn't enough ground to stop me.

If he has such extraordinary speed, like Hal Greer, that he can cut straight across and outrun the screen I've set up with my body, I have only to change my angle, cut back into the basket and I'm better off than ever. Here is one place where I would bring the behind-the-back dribble into play. The easiest way to change my angle—without exposing the ball—is to slap it behind my back from my right hand to my left.

The point I want to keep emphasizing is that the behind-the-back dribble is never used simply as a gimmick. High school coaches are always telling me they'd like to kill me, not because I originated the thing but because it has become so identified with me. Kids are great imitators, especially when something looks flashy to them, but they don't necessarily know what to imitate. They don't do it at the right time or for the right reasons.

When I go behind-the-back it is because it happens to be the best way to meet the situation of the moment and because, thank the good Lord, I was given the physical attributes to be able to do it, naturally and effortlessly.

Suppose you are driving to the basket on a 2-on-1 situation. At the beginning, you and your wingman are spread as wide as possible—I am on the right and Sam, let's say, is on the left. As we move in toward the basket, however, we begin to converge, giving the lone defensive man that much better of a chance, theoretically, to guard us both at once.

On the other hand, he is still faced with the necessity of committing himself one way or the other as soon as I hit the penetrating area. Because if he stays in the middle, I have only to keep the ball and go up and shoot.

But if he does commit himself, all I have to do is get the ball to Sam and he's under there for 2 points, uncontested. The only problem I face is that the defensive man in rushing up to me diagonally, his hands waving, and he will almost always be a much bigger man. If I try to throw an orthodox pass, I'm throwing it right through this big man with the big, waving arms, and he has a reasonable chance of deflecting it. If I try a bounce pass, he just might be able to kick it away.

All I really have to do as his body momentum is carrying him across my body is to put the ball behind my back and throw a nice little lob pass to Sam. The ball hits him as he's coming in, and there is nothing in the world this guy can possibly do to stop it.

The behind-the-back dribble, then, is used only when you have to change directions in order to avoid running into a man who is overplaying you. Most guys will change directions, under these conditions, by slapping the ball across their bodies, away from the guarding man, cutting sharply to their left and picking up their dribble at the end of their first long step.

This manages to violate two basic principles. First of all you are ignoring the cardinal rule of dribbling, which is to protect the ball at all times. You are putting the ball out there in front of you to be grabbed or deflected. When you take your step, you have to cross your legs, which is violating another basic rule.

What I do in that situation is to hesitate for one split-second in order to draw the man in to me. Then I let the ball bounce behind me in a sort of lagging motion and, reaching behind me with my right hand, slap it hard to the left. At the same time that I'm slapping it, I'm taking a long step to the left, almost a leap. With the ball behind me instead of in front of me, I have complete freedom of movement. I have such complete freedom of movement that I can even pick up the dribble with my right hand again if I want to. I have moved the man up to where he cannot possibly interfere with me after I have recovered the ball. I have succeeded in changing directions, and I have kept my body between him and the ball at all times. He can't steal it and he can't stop it. Instead of being in trouble, I am home free, because the long step, along with the element of surprise, has given me a tremendous jump on him.

But let me emphasize once more that you only do it when you are faced with that one specific situation. I've seen guys do it—and not only high school kids—when their man was playing them head on. Maybe it works and maybe it doesn't, but it doesn't accomplish a thing that couldn't have been done by an orthodox, routine fake.

What throws the kids off is that they'll also see me throwing
a behind-the-back pass on what seems to be a routine play, in a
balanced situation. But that isn't done without a purpose, either.
If, with my peripheral vision, I see that Sam is in a good position
to shoot but has only a little room, I might give him a behind-the-
back pass so as not to give away the fact that I am passing to him.
The split-second involved before his defensive man reacts is the
split-second Sam needs to get his shot away. In fact, when his man
sees me looking to the left and apparently about to pass with my
left hand, he is frequently drawn away from him.

In addition to the behind-the-back dribble and the behind-the-
back pass, there is also the behind-the-back transfer. This is also
used only on a 3-on-2 break, when you are coming down the
middle with a wingman on each side. The defensive men haven't
committed themselves yet. If they've had time to set themselves
they may even be lined up, one in back of the others, waiting for
me to tip my hand. As I hit the top of the circle, I go into the air,
putting the ball behind my back while I'm hurtling forward. As

soon as the defensive men see that ball begin to swing behind me, their automatic reaction is that I am about to pass to the man on my left. The coaching theory at this point says that the defensive man in the rear should peel over to take the man the ball is being passed to (since he has more room to go over and cover) while the front man falls back as quickly as possible and covers the other wingman to guard against a quick second pass from wing to wing.

The theory is that the very best the defense can do on a 3-on-2 break is to force the playmaker to pass, and then cut off the wingman's path to the basket. The best you can hope for is to hold them to the worst possible shot, which means you want to give them the jumper instead of the layup.

So as soon as I put the ball behind my back to start the transfer, the two defensive men just open up, leaving the center wide open for me. All I have to do is bring the ball back in front of me, while I'm still hurtling through the air, by transferring it from my right hand to my left and back in front of me. All the while, my momentum is carrying me right to the basket and I have an easy shot myself.

I will do this, again, maybe once in every twelve games and only when the situation develops precisely as I have outlined. Except that, of course, the defensive men could also be between me and the wingmen, instead of lined up in front of me.

If I tried to do it twice in a row, the front man would simply stand his ground when I put the ball behind my back. Unless my reflexes happened to be fantastically sharp, I, having committed myself, would go crashing into him. All I have done now is to nullify what should have been a sure basket and given the other team a foul shot.

Sometimes your reflexes can save you even here. About ten years ago, I was having a great game against the Knicks, partly because their backcourt was riddled by injuries and I was being covered, through much of the game by Buddy Ackerman, a first-year man who had played very little during the season. Late in the game, I was coming down the middle on a 3-on-2 break against Carl Braun and Ackerman, with Macauley in the right lane and Don Barksdale in the left. As I hit the circle, I went into the air and started the behind-the-back transfer. Braun went for Barksdale, but Ackerman came for me. At this point, I was swinging the ball back out in front of me and somehow—on pure reflex—I transferred the ball back into my right hand and kept right on swinging it. My right hand continued on behind my back for a second time, and I shot a behind-the-back pass over my shoulder to Macauley. Ackerman, finally reacting, scrambled back to cut off Macauley's path to the basket, fouled him as he was shooting and we ended up with a 3-pointer. But that's sheer reflex action, and if Ackerman had been right in front of me, I still would have barged into him.

Which brings us back to that point I made rather briefly, earlier. In all these maneuvers, you must depend upon the automatic, split-second reaction of a good, experienced, alert defensive man.

You can anticipate what a good ballplayer will do if you throw a certain fake at him, and 99 times out of 100 he will do it. If you are playing against men of lesser caliber, you can execute the most magnificent fake and get either no reaction or the wrong one. This happens all the time when I work out with the kids at my camp. I'll be making the most brilliant moves you ever saw and I'm running into kids all over the floor.

The lesson is obvious. If you have a bad defensive player on you, you should be able to do anything you want with him anyway, so do it the simple and easy way. It gets back, as always, to studying your opposition and allowing the defense to tell you, in the end, what is the best thing to do.

One last word about the behind-the-back business, and a slight footnote to my original disclaimer. I said that I have never done it just for flash. That's not altogether true. To be completely accurate, I should say that I never did it for flash in the beginning. As time went on and I discovered what a kick the customers got out of it, I would occasionally put it on display for nothing more than show, although only late in a game in which we were far ahead. It is a colorful play, and we are, in the final analysis, professional athletes being paid to entertain.

We are entertaining the L.A. fans out on the court now, all right. Russ is controlling the boards, LaRusso and Baylor aren't getting in for the second and third efforts. Baylor is being held in check. Both sides are using a lot of set plays, which is to be expected because in a game of this importance you tend to be more careful. Sam calls the 4-play, and it ends with Heinsohn turning on the foul line and putting in a jumper. With 6 minutes

and 59 seconds to go, we are leading 15-9.

The Lakers are playing well too, though, with West and LaRusso doing most of the scoring, and they put on a little streak. Wiley takes a pass with his back to the basket, leaps, turns and shoots as if he is being pressed—although Russell is nowhere near him—and pops it in to bring them to within a point of us. That's the way it goes. When he sees Russell back there, ignoring him, he takes his time, measures the shot and misses.

West puts them ahead on a fast break and the next time down the court, the rebound keeps bouncing around, giving LaRusso time to muscle in and score. I get one back with a one-hander from outside, but the Lakers come back strong. West goes up for a short jumper with Sam Jones laying all over him, and Jerry hits it while he's falling on his head. (That's the trouble with this league, all right, no defense.) With 3 minutes left in the first quarter, the Lakers are leading, 23-18.

Ramsey comes in for Heinsohn and, a few seconds later, Barnett is replacing Selvy. West goes up, as if he's shooting, but passes off to Barnett in the corner. I'm playing Dick a full man to the left, and with nowhere to go he feeds Baylor. With Elgin starting to maneuver in, I pull back to be in position to take the feed-out for the fast break. Baylor's shot bounces off the rim, comes all the way out to me and we've got it going. I'm going to feed Rams here to give him that quick shot he loves, no doubt about that. Rams drives in, hits a short one-hander, but he's called for traveling. That's the kind of a year it's been for him.

Immediately, Rams intercepts West's pass at half-court and we've got a 3-on-2. K. C. Jones, who has just come into the game for Sam, is in the right lane, so we'll give him a taste too. I work the right side, make the man commit himself, hit Case, and he narrows it to 3 points. Then another ball bounces right to me off the backboard. I spot Rams racing downcourt and throw him a long windmill pass—allowing for the right-hand slice I always get on it. Rams is right under the basket, but LaRusso is racing in on him from the other side, and he's leaping up over the basket and knocking the ball away. Goaltending, dammit! Ah, here's the whistle! Goaltending is called, and Ramsey is awarded his basket.

Barnett comes up on me with that left-handed dribble and—oh, oh—he's taking the lane I'm giving him, dribbling with his right hand. He shoots with his right hand too—what do you know about that! The shot is off, but Wiley is there to dump in the rebound. The score is 31-26.

Rams gets it right back, with a jump shot behind Russell's pick, and Rams is looking better than he's looked since the playoffs started.

Barnett takes the right-hand lane on me again, and Tommy picks him up, while I switch to LaRusso. This time, Barnett switches his dribble from his right hand back to his left hand when he's past me, and passes over to LaRusso, the smart play for him to make. Rudy jumps over me with no trouble at all, but he finally misses one of those one-handers.

I'm not tired—Oh no! It's just that I feel as if my heart is going to fall out. I know the quarter has to be about over, but the damn clock in the Sports Arena is almost impossible to see. It's too big and it hangs right down over the middle of the floor. Red and I have a signal for when I want to come out of the game. Nothing fancy. I just look over, tongue hanging out and scream something like, "Help!"

Barnett, still working on me, takes the open lane again. Sanders picks him up, leaving me with Elgin Baylor. Barnett gets the ball to Baylor, of course—you can see what strategy they've worked out—and Baylor comes muscling in on me down the middle. I don't even try to harass him. I just hold my ground, hoping I may get a charging call against him. I get banged around pretty good but the basket counts anyway.

Havlicek is coming into the game for me. As I sit down, I see there's only 38 seconds left in the quarter, and we're trailing, 33-31. I look back out to the court just in time to see Sanders tie it up with a beautiful twisting shot under the basket. But with a second to go, Jerry West is fouled in a scramble under the boards. He sinks them both, and the quarter ends with the Lakers ahead, 35-33. That gives West 15 points for the quarter. He's been killing us.

There isn't much doubt that West is the No. 2 backcourtman in the league right now. I don't think you can rate him with Robertson, though, because Jerry's not a playmaker in any sense of the

word. He'll bring the ball up the court when Selvy's out, but he won't do much more than get rid of it. Even there, you can anticipate a lot of his passes and steal a lot of balls on him. West is out there because he's a scorer and, boy, he crackles with raw ability.

Even as a scorer, though, Oscar has a better assortment of shots and is possibly a better shooter. That's hard to tell, because West looks for a jump shot from around 20 feet out, and while he hits with fantastic accuracy, his shooting average can't possibly be as high as that of a man who is always looking to drive in for a layup. Not that Jerry won't drive. He'll drive when he has his lane, and he drives very well. He plays better defense than Oscar and he rebounds a little better too.

Jerry's a raw-boned boy from West Virginia and that can sometimes lead people to think of him as a hard-nosed kid. He's quite the opposite. I have always felt that his personality hurts him a little on the court. He's too nice and he's too polite. In his rookie year (1960-61), we'd bump into each other while we were both running for the ball, and he'd kind of look shamefaced and apologize to me. Well, that isn't the attitude to have out there.

He had as mediocre a first year as a man of his ability could possibly have, because he was too self-effacing to look for his own shots. Jerry should be a gunner. Every time he gets the ball he should be looking to go to the hoop. Instead he seemed to be worried about feeding Baylor. Well, that isn't his job, it's Selvy's.

The best thing that ever happened to Jerry was when Baylor went into the service halfway through the next season. With the full scoring load thrown on him, Jerry rose to the responsibility and improved 100 percent. He's still improving. Although he likes to take his jump shot from the top of the key, he has developed to the point where he can take it from anywhere on the floor, going either to his left or right. Like all right-handers, he does prefer to be moving to his right, since that allows him to shoot off his natural body momentum. When he's moving to his left, he has to come to a stop.

Generally, then, West will be moving across the key, from the left side of the court, jumping from a 20-foot radius and hitting with disgusting regularity.

We have a special defense set up for him in the playoffs. We used it last year and we're using it again now. The Lakers' pattern with West starts with Baylor and LaRusso coming up to a medium or high pivot to take a pass from Jerry. They then have the option of looking for their own shot or giving it back to him.

If Jerry gets it back from, say, Baylor, he will swing in an arc around him, and Elgin will set a pick. If Sam Jones, who is covering West, starts to go around the pick, Jerry immediately stops in his tracks and he's got the open 20-foot jump shot he's looking for. If Sam fights over the pick, Jerry continues to swing around Elgin for a couple of more steps, moving away from the pick, and since he can hit from anywhere on that arc, he's still got his open 20-foot jumper.

The only way we can combat it is to have Sam apply as much pressure on him for as long as possible. As soon as Sanders, who is covering Baylor, sees the pick developing, Satch will shout, "Switch," and cut across to cover Jerry himself. We have now removed the pick and made it necessary for West to try to jump over a big and agile man.

Baylor's move, of course, is to go for the basket. He has a much smaller man covering him, and the routine play would be for West to lob him a high pass. But this is a fairly difficult pass to make, especially since Baylor isn't *that* big. As a matter of fact, this is the play we hope he will try (with either Baylor or La-Russo), because Jerry just isn't that clever with the ball. (Try it on Robertson and he'll kill you with it.)

Jerry will generally do one of two things. He has an excellent head-and-shoulder fake. The big men, who are not used to seeing it, think he is going up for his jump shot, so they jump up too, arms waving. As they start to come down, Jerry goes up into them, timing it so that the arms of the big man will almost have to foul him. He's strong enough so that he can get his shot off anyway, and he picks up a lot of 3-point plays.

After a while, the big men get used to it, though, and what happens is that the switch just stops the play, and the Lakers start all over again.

As has been customary all year, I'm on the bench as the second period starts. We start off fast with Heinsohn getting a complete breakaway from the tap, and tying it up, 35-35. Then Russ goes way up for Barnett's rebound, and Tommy hits a jumper at the other end to put us ahead.

Tommy bats the ball away from LaRusso as Rudy tries to drive around him, and Ramsey scores. Even on the bench, we can feel the momentum gathering. Barnett, still taking that right-hand lane, drives on Case, shifting to his left hand to shoot. He misses the shot, and Havlicek and Case are down on a fast break, which ends with Havlicek sinking a jump shot from the

side. John is running well. For the first time in the series he's having no trouble with the ankle.

We have hit on our first four shots. The Lakers call time out to give us a chance to cool off.

When play is resumed, Jim Krebs comes into the game for the first time.

We lose the ball for the first time in the quarter when Ramsey gets called for traveling.

The Lakers score their first points of the quarter when Rams, who has the job of covering Baylor now that Sanders is resting, fouls him as he's wheeling for that work-in shot of his. Elgin sinks them both.

Shortly afterward, K.C. comes driving across the circle, swerves into Baylor and picks up a foul-shot for himself. That's a trick of Case's. He's worked it beautifully here, and he's worked it on a tough man.

What Case does is to come up the court after he's taken an outlet pass, angling out across the center. The big man—and Case will usually pick on the man guarding Russell—will be lumbering back through the middle. Case comes up alongside him—with a couple of strides of space in between them laterally—and then slices right back in toward him. The big man, unable to untrack himself and too tall to slap the ball away, practically falls right over him. It's a good play if you don't mind having a giant fall on you. I've never felt the urge myself.

K. C. Jones is usually identified as "no relation to Sam," since Sam's name has usually been mentioned first. That in itself tells a lot about Case's position with the team. For seven years, he has been playing in my shadow—just as Sam was originally in the position of being overshadowed by both Sharman and me. Case's situation is slightly different than Sam's ever was, because he doesn't have his nonrelative's overwhelming ability. To some degree, Case has been a specialist for us. He does everything on a basketball floor except shoot.

For the past two years, though, he has been playing about as much as I have. Next year, when he gets his chance to replace me as playmaker, we're going to find out if he can be a full-time player in this league. If he can't, there will always be the question of whether he could have made it if he hadn't been forced to spend so much time on the bench in those early years.

I think he can do it. There is no doubt at all that he's a good enough passer to do the job. Not a great job, but a good one. His trouble at the moment is that he has completely lost his confidence in his shooting and, as I have said, you cannot be a playmaker unless you're also a scoring threat. Case refuses to look at the basket, and unless he understands that he must shoot in order to move the defense he'll end up 15 feet from the basket with nobody to pass to.

While nobody has ever accused him of being a great shooter, he is an adequate shooter.

K.C.'s personality, like West's, doesn't lend itself easily to taking charge, to asserting himself as a shooter. Among the players and among his friends, he relaxes and becomes not only extrovertive but quite entertaining. He sings very well and he's a marvelous pantomimist. He will imitate other players in the league, and he has the ability to develop simply remarkable facial resemblances. Walter Dukes has a peculiar way of jutting out his chin and lips, and a peculiar stride—as if he is walking uphill—and Case has it all down to perfection.

He and Russell will sit in front of a television set, commenting back-and-forth on a commercial, and on a good day they will become so hilarious that you'd swear it was a prepared routine.

Among strangers, though, K.C. is not only quiet, he is silent and completely withdrawn.

There is one thing that tends to make me feel that Case will rise to the opportunity. He does play an aggressive, confident, tough, harassing defense. If I were sure he'd be able to carry that same aggressiveness over to the offense, I'd have no qualms about him. But as a playmaker, he has to be mentally aggressive as well. The playmaker has to say *I'm in charge here*. Well, Russell will hammer these points home to him, and Case listens to Russ.

Out on the floor, the game has turned sloppy, something I hate to see. Both sides are running helter-skelter, up and down on disorganized fast breaks, losing the ball, throwing it away, missing shots. West is coming down now on a 3-on-1 break, with Russell the lone defender, retreating nicely, fending them off. West, waiting for Russ to commit himself, comes in too deep and now Russ fakes a move, shifts quickly, eats up the ground between himself and West with one great stride and bats down West's shot with a big hand. The crowd moans.

Russ has recovered the ball too. He passes to Havlicek, and John is racing down the floor as players are trying to reverse their direction all around him. John stops at the foul line, jumps and hits.

With the period half over, LaRusso sinks a one-hander from the corner, the first Laker basket of the period. We are leading, 45-39, and still on the move. Russ moves over to help Ramsey with Baylor, Baylor flips the outlet pass to Krebs. And, hey, Russ fools them by coming out to Krebs and blocking his shot.

210

They try it again a couple of minutes later, and this time Russ just stands under the basket and lets Krebs shoot. With all the time in the world, Krebs tries to make it too good and misses.

Russ is blocking everything out there. He blocks Barnett's shot on a drive, feeds it off to K.C. and Case leads a 3-on-2 break. As Case is down the middle, the two Laker defenders are trying to make him commit himself, confident he's looking to pass. *Go in, Case!* Case splits them through the middle and is up for the layup. That will give them something to think about.

We're leading, 57-47, when time is called. There's 2 minutes and 46 seconds to go. Red tells me to go in for K.C. I throw the jacket off my shoulders and go to the scorer's table to report. In theory, you're reporting to the scorekeeper; actually you're reporting to the announcer sitting just alongside him. He wants to know who you're replacing so he can make the announcement as soon as you run on the floor. In keeping with the accepted practice, I don't say, "Cousy for Jones," I just say, "Jones."

Play resumes and I find myself just where I was before I went out, covering Baylor on a switch. The result is the same too. Elgin powers around me—have you ever felt a freight car rush past?—for the basket.

We come back up, and I have a long one-hand set shot. I take it off the wrong foot and it's up, over and in.

West misses at the other end, and we're off and running on the fast break. My first glance catches Heinsohn digging behind me as a trailer. As I hit penetrating territory, I catch a blur of green behind me and, knowing that it's Tommy, I flip the ball back over my head. Tommy's shot misses, bounces around. Havlicek has it, goes up in the mob under the basket, misses. But Satch drives in from the corner, times his leap perfectly and tips in the rebound. We have a basket because both our forwards have run and dug and battled. The score is 61-49. We have 12 points, and everything is going right for us. We can smell the championship. Russ feeds and picks nicely for Rams, who scores.

I give Russ a bounce pass under, and, oh boy, Wiley is all over him. Russ makes the first foul, and it's 13 points. He misses the second, though. Everybody in front of me is jumping and—what have we here?—the ball is off everybody's hands and back out to me. I step into a nice open pocket and I have a nice soft one-hander. We're 15 points ahead.

I give one of those back nicely by fouling Selvy. Back we come, though. Into Russell on the high post, back to me, a bounce pass to Rams. Ramsey shoots it right back to me and I have an alley down the middle. I'm through and I'm up and we have 16 points with only seconds left in the first half. I've got three fast baskets; 16 points for the half. I'm going out with the whole bit; the world's championship and a good game.

West, who had been stopped cold by K.C., gets one of his typical baskets just before the gun. A one-hand jump shot, riding on Havlicek's back.

The half ends, and we're leading, 66-52.

The passage out to the locker room is through a roped-off exit, behind the basket. In L.A., the fans are no real problem. If the Lakers had been ahead we could have expected a few choice insults to be hurled at Arnold. Under these conditions, the anti-Auerbach brigade can only maintain a sullen silence. The shouts to me are all friendly, and even neighborly: "Hey, Cooz, how's

Worcester?" and "Holy Cross '50, Cooz!" and "How's everything at Scollay Square?" *There's* a guy who's been away a long time. Scollay Square is, at the moment, a vacant lot. He's never heard of urban redevelopment?

What's there for Arnold to say to us back in the locker room except to tell us to keep up the good work. Buddy is bent over Havlicek, asking him about the ankle, and John is nodding in obvious satisfaction. He and Case and Rams have been great. There's the Celtics bench again. When the bench is keeping that pressure on, we have no problems.

The L.A. statistician comes in to hand Red the sheet with the first-half figures. Red will check the scoring and the shooting percentages but, most of all, he will check the fouls to see if anybody is in trouble. If one of us has three fouls, he'll warn him to watch himself. If anybody has four fouls, Red will probably hold him out at the start. He also wants to check the Lakers' fouls, so that if any of their men are in trouble we can direct the attack at them.

We've hit 55 percent of our shots in the first half, a tremendous average. There's no doubt we've been taking our best shots. We've had 52 shots to their 43, which shows Russell is controlling the backboard nicely.

Sam Jones has only one basket and one foul, I hadn't noticed that. That's a surprise. Sam has been our big scorer this year. In the playoffs, he's been averaging 25 points. Normally, I'd be aware of that kind of fall-off from Sam, or any of our scorers, because I'd want to make sure he was getting his opportunities. In this one, there's no thinking of tomorrow. You got to go with the guys who are doing well. With K.C., Havlicek and me all shooting so well, I haven't had to look to get production out of another backcourtman.

Sam Jones was a surprise first-draft choice in 1956, at a time when nobody had heard of either him or his school, North Carolina College, and we hardly seemed to be in desperate need of another backcourtman. He wasn't even graduating that year. Bill Mokray our promotional director, had picked up information somewhere that Sam was something special and that he was eligible for the draft because his original college class was about to graduate.

When Sharman left, Sam stepped right in and took over. Offensively, he is probably the toughest guard in the league to play, because he's lightning fast and has all the moves and all the shots. He is also tall, 6′4″, and he can jump up to the roof. Now that I'm leaving, people will finally stop looking upon Sam as the other guard and he will be making the All-Star team regularly. He has already moved right in alongside Robertson and West as one of the three top guards in basketball.

His touch is so good that he rates just below Oscar Robertson in scoring percentage, even though almost all of Sam's shots are from outside. A good percentage of them are 25-foot jumpers, which in today's game is considered about as far outside as you can get. Sam's other trademark is that he's about the last of the players who regularly uses the backboard to bank in side shots.

With his speed and his shooting ability, it would be belaboring the obvious to add that he's a handy man to have with you on the fast break.

Sam is a soft-spoken, easy-going man who just seems to go along and do his job. On the surface, at least, there is none of the deep-seated rage that you find in Russell. Sam had never left North Carolina until he came North to play with us. Like most Negroes who have spent their entire life in the South, he had apparently already made his accommodations or, at least, had developed his façade.

Sam's play is the 2-play, and it is one of our bread-and-butter plays. As Sam hits the penetrating area, he passes to one of the forwards—let's say, Heinsohn—who has come up to meet him, bringing his defensive man along. Sam immediately moves off to the side of the court that Heinsohn has just cleared, moving all the way over to the baseline, just about even with the foul line, if the foul line were to be extended all the way across the floor. Heinsohn now whips the ball back to Sam and keeps moving to the other side of the floor, clearing his old area.

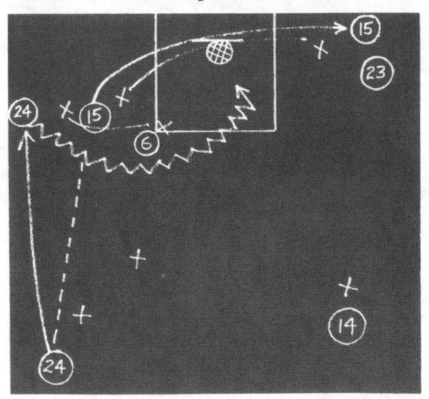

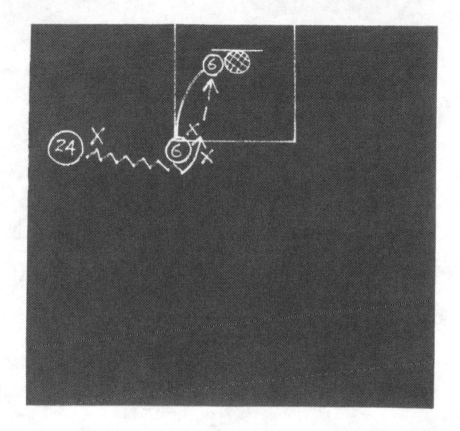

Meanwhile, Bill Russell is moving to a high-post position so that Sam can swing back out to the middle and go around him.

Normally, Sam will just wheel around Russ, using his body as a screen, and either drive down the middle or, if his defensive man is cutting in front of Russ, take his jump shot which, with Sam, is more effective than my layup.

After this happens a couple of times, Sam's man will usually start anticipating that middle drive as soon as the play starts to develop and he will overplay Sam toward the middle to try to cut him off. So instead of driving for the middle, Sam makes a quick fake toward the middle and goes baseline on him, either driving down and under, or taking his jump shot from the side.

The other defense is to eliminate the pick by switching Russell's man to Sam as he is driving for the middle. Now it is up to Russ to react and head for the basket. Sam just stops at the line and gives Russ the high lob pass for what should be an easy dunk shot.

Everybody's in high spirits in the locker room. The smell of the championship is in the room, stronger than the liniment. The shouts are high-pitched and happy:

"Dammit, we've gone this far, let's make sure we don't lose it now."

"Everybody stays on their toes out there. We're not in yet."

And most of all it's: "Let's keep running."

We say it a hundred different times in a dozen different ways. Keep moving! Keep moving! Keep moving! "This is a running team. If we stop, we're dead."

So we go back out there for the second half and *stop running!*

Give Schaus some credit. Freddie has thrown all his height into the starting lineup by pulling Baylor out to the backcourt and packing Ellis and LaRusso at the forwards, with Wiley at center. What surprises me most is that he had done the same thing in the All-Star game, with Chamberlain, Bellamy and Pettit, and we had just run them off their feet. You don't get something without giving up something, and when you pack the lineup with that much height you're giving up speed and agility and coordination.

It's a radical strategy for this kind of a game; still, in the all-or-nothing-at-all spot he's in now, he's got to do something. It's a good enough gamble.

Worried? Who's worried. Speed and agility, that's what we're famous for. Red switches me on to West, and all Sam has to do is cover Baylor.

The half starts with Russell backing off to let Wiley shoot. Ellis gets the rebound, Russ goes to him, blocks the shot but fouls him. Ellis sinks them both. The height has helped them there, all right.

They score again when LaRusso's one-hander from the left side ticks in off the backboard. Rudy doesn't use the backboard on that shot. That could have been a lucky one. Luck or not, they've picked up a fast four points.

The scoring alternates for the next 6 minutes, with our lead shifting back and forth between 10 and 7 points. And yet, they're playing better ball than we are, and I know it. The psychological factor has moved in again. Those big men have got us concentrating so much on getting those rebounds that once we do get the ball we're not geared to break. We've got that good lead, and despite all our half-time chatter—and against our best resolve

and obvious self-interest—we've gone into this cautious, patterned style of play that always kills us. I'm shouting for everybody to run, and I'm *walking* up the court with the ball myself.

With 7 minutes to go, Wiley tries to clear a ball out from under the basket. I move in to the top of the circle, a little to the left

of center, and intercept it. I have a good angle coming in to the basket, but Jerry West comes up quickly to my right-hand side, blocking off my shot. I shift the ball to my left hand, and take a long, sweeping left-handed hook shot from about 15 feet out, and—swish—it's in. I haven't made many shots like that in

my life; I haven't even taken many. The boys give me the business as we're running back: "Are you kiddin' me, baby?" they call out. "You got to be kidding!"

The Lakers are playing the slow, set game they have to with their big men, and that's tending to settle the whole game into this slow tempo, too. We can't break out of it. Baylor and West are hitting consistently from the outside.

West holds up a set play again as he comes down with the ball. It's LaRusso coming up high, taking the pass and giving it back to Jerry. Jerry starts to wheel in his arc around LaRusso's pick. Only this time he stops, fakes as if he's going to drive straight in, then feeds off to LaRusso, who has slipped over to the foul line. Rudy turns to face the basket and pops in that one-hander again. Our lead has dwindled to 6 points.

Now West has Wiley all alone in the corner, as Russ continues to camp under the middle. Jerry decides to take the shot himself. He misses, but Baylor has the ball, passes out to LaRusso on the foul line, and this time Rudy leaps high and hits a one-hand jump. The score is 79-75, and I'm screaming for time out. They've

picked up 10 points on us in 7 minutes.

Red's hands are on his hips, his head is bobbing up and down. He is far calmer than I am, though. I'm screaming and I'm cursing and I'm using language that goes back to my kids days on the East Side. I barely know what I'm saying. "What the _____ is going on here? *We're not running!* We work a whole half to build up a lead and we're _____ it away in a few minutes. We got to run!

Nobody's moving out there! Nobody!"

We come back running. The saliva is flowing. We're not putting anything together yet, but at least we're moving. With 3 minutes and 18 seconds to go, Ramsey takes a bounce pass as he's driving in and pulls us 6 points ahead.

West comes back up the floor. I see him looking to pass off to the right, so I back off him fast, intercept, and I've got Sanders

and Havlicek with me. I kick it to Sanders on the side, and he hits Havlicek, who is driving in from the other side. It's now 8 points, with 3:07 to go, and this is more like it.

I'm belted under the other basket, and by the time I look up, Ellis is scoring.

But Russell is up to stuff in Havlicek's rebound at the other end, and it's 8 again.

Russ gets the rebound off the defensive board too, and Havlicek has it on a 3-on-2 fast break. John works the left-hand side, but West throws a fake at him, turns beautifully and blocks the pass. But things are working out for us now. The ball bounces right to Ramsey, and when Rams blows the shot too, Sanders is there again to tip it in. There's 1:44 to go and we're 10 points ahead.

West misses his jump shot, and the rebound drops right down into my lap. I come up the center, bounce a pass to Havlicek, and John puts the ball in the hole.

The Lakers yell for time with 1:26 left. In less than 2 minutes, our lead has jumped from 4 points to 12 points.

Arnold sits me down during the time out. and sends in K. C. Jones. The third period ends with no further scoring.

As the fourth period starts, Schaus has Barnett and Krebs in the game. If I want to second-guess, I have to say he should have pulled the big guys out of there when he got the lead down to 4 points. Of course, I also have to admit that if the Lakers had gone on to win with those big men, I'd be calling him the genius of the ages. Still and all, his purpose had been to catch us off balance and put the Lakers back into the game. When the lead was cut to 4 points, his strategy had served its purpose. That was the time to go back to the starting lineup.

Barnett scores immediately from a scramble in front of the basket. Sanders is fouled, and I go back into the game. Only 49 seconds have been played in the quarter. West is bringing the ball up, so I move over to cover Barnett. I'm running backwards easily. Barnett cuts sharply to the right, I cut with him—*and I'm sitting on the floor!* I'm sitting on the floor with nobody near me, and there's an excruciating pain shooting up the inside of my left ankle. It hurts so bad that I roll over onto my right side to take all weight off it.

The players are coming back to me, and I'm rolling back and forth it hurts so much. Buddy LaRoux is leaning over, talking

234

to me. At last, I'm pulled up, and I'm limping off the court, supported by Buddy on one side and Loscutoff on the other. I had been back in the game for exactly 14 seconds.

They help me to the far end of the bench, near the basket we're shooting at. I sit at the very end, my back to the other players, the leg extended straight out in front of me. What a way to end the whole career; sitting on the bench with the first ankle injury of my life. Dr. Ernie Vanderweghe, the old Knick star, has come down to look at it. His fingers explore the ankle and he's asking me to twist and turn it so he can find out whether anything's

broken. "Where do you feel the pain?" he asks me.

And, funny thing, I can't feel any pain anymore. As soon as I sat down the pain had gone. Boy, he must be thinking I was putting on a pretty good act out there, rolling around and everything. A real farewell performance. When in Hollywood do as the natives do.

"It's numb," Vanderweghe says. "You've probably got a bad sprain."

I'm paying more attention to Vanderweghe than to the game, and yet I'm aware that everything he's doing and saying is being punctuated by staccato bursts of cheering from the stands. It's the kind of cheering, rising steadily in excitement and volume, that you get when the home team is picking up momentum. I keep twisting my head around to try to see the action on the Laker's side of the court where everything seems to be happening. I'm not really that concerned, though. I'm under the impression, somehow, that the game is almost over and we've got it in the bag.

Buddy is packing the foot in ice to stop the swelling and numb the ankle even more. He lays a wet towel filled with ice on the floor, and he places my foot inside it. When that begins to cool off, he has another, larger ice-pack ready. This time, he wraps it completely around the top of my foot. I tell him there's still no pain, so he dries it off and gets ready to put on a special strapping he uses for foot sprains. I'm allergic to Benzoine, the skin adherent usually used, however, so he has to spray some special kind of liquid all along my foot. The coolness feels good against it.

He bandages the ankle as tightly as he can to immobilize it. The crowd is roaring constantly now, and I keep craning my neck to see what's happening.

Buddy has strapped the ankle so tight that it's as if it were in a cast. He helps me to my feet, and I bounce up and down on the ankle, gingerly, to test it. It feels just fine.

On the court, right in front of me, the Celtics are lining up for an in-bound play. Sanders is holding the ball under the basket.

Three men from each side are lined up along the foul lane just in front of him, the offensive men outside the lane marker, the defensive men inside.

Sanders slaps the ball to signal the start of the play. Sam Jones, our lone man behind the circle, fakes as if to come in. Havlicek, the rear man in the line peels off to his left. Heinsohn, just in front of Havlicek, waits a beat and cuts sharply to the right. Russell, who has been standing in front of Heinsohn steps back just enough to put a brush block on LaRusso.

On an in-bound play, nobody can switch men, because it's all happening too close to the basket. If a defensive man switched, the man he was supposed to be covering would automatically break for the basket, take a little flip and sink an easy hoop. All in-bound plays are one-pass, one-shot plays.

Tommy gets the pass, takes the shot and misses. But Baylor has rushed over to bother him, and he fouls him trying to box him away from the rebound. Tommy has a foul shot, and he misses.

With the play moving upcourt, I start walking up toward Red. I glance up at the clock to catch the score—*and I can't believe it!* I have to look twice. I still can't believe it.

The score is 100-99. Our lead is down to 1 point.

As I'm walking toward Red, I ask myself, for the first time, whether I can go back out there. I don't really think I can play on this ankle, but I do think my presence on the court might give the boys a lift. The Lakers are gathering momentum, and when it starts late like this on your own home court, it can very easily carry through to the end of the game. Yes, I decide, it's worth taking a chance that my return will shake things up, will change the whole psychological atmosphere.

This is the time they need somebody to assume the responsibilities of a playmaker. They're used to having me in there, bringing up the ball and calling the plays. It's important psychologically that they feel everything's in its place and everyone's doing their job. I don't have to get into the action, all I have to do is take the ball up the court and be ready to run back again. If I can't run, they can get me out of there in a hurry.

As I say, it isn't thought out that logically, step by step. It's thought out, not in a jumble really but in one chunk. I can't do too much harm. If we lose, there's still another game to go. (I

don't have to worry about what I'd be thinking if this were the seventh game. It isn't the seventh game.)

Red is at the other end of the long bench, as far away from me as he can be. The play is at the Laker side of the court and his back is turned to me. West has fouled Sam Jones. That means the ball is dead and I can be sent right into the game. It's make up my mind right now. It's now or not at all.

Red stands up when he sees me coming toward him. "How does it feel?"

"Well," I tell him, "I think I can go."

He looks at me briefly and nods. "Go in for Havlicek," he says.

He doesn't give me any pep talk. He doesn't even say, "Go get 'em, Cooz." He just nods, because we've been together long enough so that he's willing to take my word for it. There's enough excitement all around us so that we don't have to put on any performance. The excitement and tension is so strong on our bench that you can feel it crackling in the air. Besides, Arnold's got nine other things he's thinking about at this stage of the game.

I report to the scoring table: "Havlicek."

(The strange part—or not so strange if you can appreciate how time telescopes and bends in an emotional game like this—is that I would have sworn afterward that I had hurt my ankle halfway through the final period, spent no more than 2 or 3 minutes of actual game time—7 or 8 minutes overall—getting the ankle frozen and taped, and returned to the game with less than two minutes to go. The records show, of course, that I left after 1:03 of the fourth quarter and returned with 4:43 still remaining.)

I come in and there's no joyous greetings, no fight talk. No one asks me how the ankle feels. These are all professionals. If I'm out here they're willing to assume I can do the job.

Sam misses his foul shot. Baylor gets the rebound and I retreat straight down the floor, not cutting at all. It feels all right. West misses his jumper, and Russell has it.

Sam brings it up, and the ball goes to Sanders, off in the right-hand corner. Satch looks to pass off as Baylor puts pressure on him; he can't find anybody and just to get rid of it, he puts it over his head and takes a hurried 2-hand shot to the basket. It hardly hits the nets as it swishes through. 102-99.

I'm still running straight up and down, but now the ball goes to Barnett in the corner, and he slaps it behind his back with his left hand and picks it up with his right, possibly to test my ankle. I cut hard, and it hurts a little, but no more than a twinge. I've cut off his path with that cut, because he's backed against the outside line. He passes off, but the ball goes loose and Heinsohn picks it up. Tommy kicks it out to me. I'm up the left side of the court and I cut to the right—off that left foot—without thinking, and dribble up the middle. Sanders is cutting under the basket, I give him a nice bounce pass, and he's in for the score. We're leading, 104-99, with 3:32 to go.

The Lakers call time out. In the huddle, we're all excited, everybody's yelling now, inspiring each other. As we break to go back on the court, it suddenly occurs to me, for some reason, that I don't know how many fouls are on me. I turn back to the scorer's table. There are four.

The Lakers get a freak basket when Russ, leaping high above the basket for a rebound, accidentally tips it in. When was the last time I saw that happen? The lead is now down to 3.

Baylor sinks a foul shot, and it's down to 2.

West has been covering me, and so far he hasn't pressed me when I'm coming down with the ball. That was something I'd been afraid of, that he'd pick me up in the backcourt and press me all the way down to put the ankle to the test. I'm just going up and down the court as I had hoped. If it were K. C. Jones, he'd be putting the question to me all right.

I come down the right-hand side and bounce a pass to Sanders, who's directly in front of me. Oh, oh, it bounces right out of his hands. Satch looked as if he might have lost sight of it.

There's 2:30 to go.

West calls a set play coming down. Barnett cuts sharply on me, and as I cut with him, I feel the sharp stab of pain. Bad. West has passed off to LaRusso, and Rudy passes—*Good boy, Tommy!* Tommy had fallen back off LaRusso, and he's grabbed the ball and he's driving through to the basket all by himself. He's up and the ball is in. The lead is back to 4 points, and that was a big play.

The crowd has gone absolutely silent.

My ankle hurts, and I'm wondering whether this isn't the time to take myself out of here. But the play goes on, carrying me upcourt with it. I'm limping a little, but the pain is receding.

Wiley is fouled. His shot goes in and out. That one looked as if it were halfway down the netting. We're getting the breaks

again. We're going to win this.

I'm straight upcourt again with the ball. The pain has almost left. I pass to Russell in the high-post, and West falls back to double-team him. He's got the message that he doesn't have to worry about my going into the action. Russ tries to drive around Jerry and loses control of the ball.

There's 1:48 to go.

Barnett takes me into the right-hand corner again. Again, West gets the ball to him. This time I anticipate he's going to drive to the right, so I try to surprise him by making a sudden, diagonal lunge for the ball. Barnett's too clever with the ball for that. He pulls it away, twists around me to the left and he has his jump shot. It's way off, and Tommy has the rebound.

I come back slower, yelling for the others to move the ball around. We're in good shape. With time running out, we'll either kill some time or lure the Lakers into a foul. The Lakers are careful not to foul us, and with the 24-second time limit almost run out, I step inside the foul line for the first time since I've come back, take a pass from Tommy and get the shot off just as the 24-second horn in sounding. I know it's off all the way. It hits the right-hand rim and bounces away.

There is 1:12 left.

Baylor drives in on the other end of the court and knocks the lead down to 106-104.

Time remaining: 1:07.

We move the ball around again. At one point I find myself taking a pass under the basket. I send it right back out to Russell. Russ flips it to Sam, gives him a pick, and Sam hits his one-handed jump. It's only Sam's second basket and fifth point of the day. He picked the right time for it.

We are 4 points up, with only 45 seconds to go.

But not for long. Barnett takes that open lane to the right and drives along the baseline, shifting the ball to his left hand as he goes. As Russ moves to him, Barnett fakes his shot beautifully. Russ goes up, and Barnett is driving underneath him, still tight-roping the baseline. He turns back on the other side of the basket and sinks a twisting shot. Russ, recovering as only he can, has spun around and shot out his right hand to try to block it from the other side. The arm hits Barnett on the shoulder as he's twisting in, and he has a foul to go with the basket.

Barnett goes to the foul line and finishes off the 3-point play. Just like that, our lead is back down to 1 point. The roof is coming off the place.

We take time out.

There are 33 seconds left in the game.

I'm bringing the ball up again, and we need this one. Sam is cutting off behind me, so I flip it over my shoulder to him as I hit the foul line. Sam passes to Tommy on the left and drives in. I'm moving into the slot just to the right of the foul line again. Tommy kicks it in to Sam, and Sam kicks it over to me, and I step in for a nice soft one-hander. The ball leaves my hand perfectly. I'm sure it's in. But, damn, it drifts off to the left at the last second and it's bouncing high off the rim.

But Tommy is going high too, and he has it, and Wiley racks him as he's trying to go back up for the shot.

Tommy has won it for us once with the interception. Win it for us again, Tommy.

He studies the basket, takes a deep breath and sinks the first one.

He studies the basket, takes a deep breath and sinks the second one.

The score is 110-107.

There are 20 seconds to go.

Barnett has me in that corner again. He fakes as if he's going down the baseline, then wheels completely around, turning his back to me. He shifts the ball to his left hand as he's jumping, and gets the shot off fast. No good. Russell and Baylor are battling for the rebound. The whistle blows. Jump ball.

There are 13 seconds left.

Red is yelling for a time out. "Don't give them a 3-pointer," he tells us. "A basket isn't going to hurt us, just don't give them a 3-pointer."

The ball bounces to Heinsohn from the jump, and LaRusso charges into him as he's trying to get his shot away. It's the seventh foul of the period for Los Angeles, and Tommy will get a penalty shot. Three chances to make two fouls. There is an absolute silence in the arena . . . an absolute and eerie silence.

He makes the first, misses the second, and uses the penalty shot to give us a 112-107 lead.

There are 10 seconds left.

It's over now, and I can feel the rising excitement that takes hold of you when you know you've got it in the bag, and it's just a matter of playing out the last few seconds. There is a prickly feeling all over my body. It's over.

Barnett starts to spin around me again, decides not to waste the time, and just throws the ball up toward the basket. It's off the rim, and Baylor is up to dunk in the rebound. Who cares? It's over.

There are only 3 or 4 seconds to go.

I wait for Sam to throw me the ball from out of bounds, take 3 or 4 long, leaping strides upcourt and, I don't know why, just heave the ball up to the rafters. I jump up and down, and time is running out while the ball is descending. Ankle? What ankle?

Russell is leaping over our bench to get the ball on a big bounce. I've forgotten in my excitement that I want this last ball as a souvenir. Now Russ is running up to me with the ball cradled in his arm, and I'm jumping on his back. Somebody else has Russ by the back of the hair. Red is pushing his head in between Russ and me. Russ is enveloping us all with that huge wing span of his, one hand gripping the back of Sanders' neck, the other hung over K.C.'s shoulder.

It's over, and we won it all. It's all over. It's over.

We're into the locker room, screaming. It's all exhilaration now, with no room left for even the slightest twinge of nostalgia that I will never be here again as a player, as one of the boys. From now on, it will be one foot in and one foot out, the old grad returning to the classroom. But I've got both feet in now. No room for nostalgia now. No nostalgia wanted.

Russ gives me the ball. "You were a tiger tonight, baby."

"You feel like crying again, Bob?" a reporter asks hopefully.

Cry, hell! I feel like cheering. "I'd cry for you," Russell tells him, "but I'm too big and ugly to cry."

We're supposed to catch a jet right out, thank the Lord. There'll be a champagne party on the plane. I could use some right now though. I'm parched.

There's not a can of beer in the place. They had thought we'd be running for the airport, so nobody had thought to have any beer sent in.

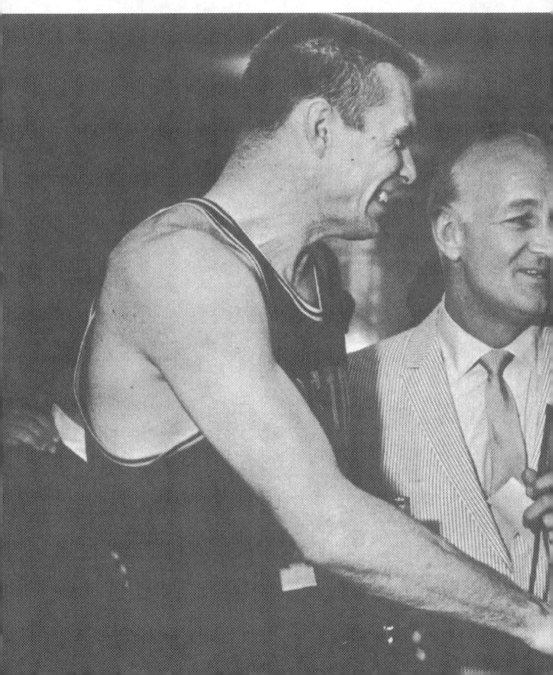

There are questions to be answered before we leave, though, and pictures to be posed for. Television cameras have been set up.

Tommy Harmon has his TV camera set up in the locker room and I'm called to go on with him.

I'm running to Buddy to ask if he can please find me a can of beer somewhere. The more I can't get it, the more I want it.

Never in my life have I been this thirsty.

Somebody shouts in that Bob Wolff wants me back out on the floor for a television interview. The auditorium is almost completely empty as I come out. I have never seen an auditorium empty so quickly. Even the crowd that is always gathered around the TV camera is small, and the people all seem stunned. They cannot believe that we have really beaten their Lakers.

Bob has begun to interview Red Auerbach as I arrive. The best bet of the night is that Arnold is going to say, "I guess Los Angeles isn't the basketball capital of the world yet."

"I guess Los Angeles isn't the basketball capital of the world yet," Arnold says. "We didn't do too bad for a bunch of old men."

Old feuders never die, they only crow away. Good old Arnold. I'd kiss him except we're on national TV and he might hit me.

They're holding the plane for us, we're told, but they're not going to hold it forever.

We finally shake loose and rush for the airport. As the plane leaves the ground, circles and heads east, Russell looks down and

says gleefully, ". . . and as the basketball capital of the world sinks slowly into the sunset, we can only say, 'Good-bye, Los Angeles. Good-bye, to the basketball capital of the world.'"

Mayor Collins of Boston is there with an entourage to greet us as we land at Logan Airport in the morning. My ankle has tightened up so much that I can barely stand. The funny thing is that it's the outside of the ankle that hurts now, not the inside. All the ligaments have been torn.

My car is at the airport, where I left it, but it seems advisable to let Tommy do the driving. At Lake Bridge, just before Worcester, we're met by a police escort. The committee for the Worcester Day affair has brought our wives and kids out to meet us, and Tommy and I are to ride home with our families in special cars. "Watch the weight next year," I tell Tommy, as we part. Old habits die hard.

If I had any shame I'd be embarrassed. It couldn't have worked out better. I had a good year, the team won the championship and—to be honest—the torn ligaments and the return to the game lent the final Hollywood flourish. People like to embellish a good story, and I now find that everybody seems to think I came limping back, my face contorted with pain, and dragged myself up and down the court, scoring key baskets.

I made only one contribution the whole time I was in there, the pass that set up Sanders right after I came back into the game. After that, my only contribution was my physical presence. Maybe it helped, and maybe it didn't. Who's to say we wouldn't have won by 10 points if I'd stayed on the bench.

Even my last basket worked out perfectly. If you remember, it was that left-handed hook shot early in the third period. If a kind genie had given me the choice of the type of shot I'd want for my final basket, that's what it would have been. Frankly, I wouldn't have thought I'd have the guts to take that kind of a shot in that kind of a game, let alone make it.

I mean, it isn't that vital when you stack it up alongside everything else that has happened in thirteen years, but it's a nice thing to remember.

272

CAREER HIGHLIGHTS

BOB COUSY

Born August 9, 1928. Height 6.1 Weight 175.

Alma Mater—Holy Cross '50.

Sea.—Team	G.	Min.	FGA.	FGM.	Pct.	FTA.	FTM.	Pct.	Reb.	Ast.	PF.	Disq.	Pts.	Avg.
50-51—Boston	69	....	1138	401	.352	365	276	.756	474	341	185	2	1078	15.6
51-52—Boston	66	2681	1388	512	.369	506	409	.808	421	441	190	5	1433	21.7
52-53—Boston	71	2945	1320	464	.352	587	479	.816	449	547	227	4	1407	19.8
53-54—Boston	72	2857	1262	486	.385	522	411	.787	394	518	201	3	1383	19.2
54-55—Boston	71	2747	1316	522	.397	570	460	.807	424	557	165	1	1504	21.2
55-56—Boston	72	2767	1223	440	.360	564	476	.844	492	642	206	2	1356	18.8
56-57—Boston	64	2364	1264	478	.378	442	363	.821	309	478	134	0	1319	20,6
57-58—Boston	65	2222	1262	445	.353	326	277	.850	322	463	136	1	1167	18.0
58-59—Boston	65	2403	1260	484	.384	385	329	.855	359	557	135	0	1297	20.0
59-60—Boston	75	2588	1481	568	.383	403	319	.791	352	715	146	2	1455	19.4
60-61—Boston	76	2564	1382	513	.371	452	352	.779	331	591	196	0	1378	18.1
61-62—Boston	75	2116	1181	462	.391	333	251	.754	261	584	135	0	1175	15.7
62-63—Boston	76	1976	988	392	.397	298	219	.735	201	515	175	0	1003	13.2
Totals	917	30230	16465	6167	.375	5753	4621	.803	4789	6949	2231	20	16955	18.5

PLAYOFF RECORD

Sea.—Team	G.	Min.	FGA.	FGM.	Pct.	FTA.	FTM.	Pct.	Reb.	Ast.	PF.	Disq.	Pts.	Avg.
50-51—Boston	2	....	42	9	.214	12	10	.833	15	12	8	....	28	14.0
51-52—Boston	3	138	65	26	.400	44	41	.932	12	19	13	1	93	31.0
52-53—Boston	6	270	120	46	.383	73	61	.836	25	37	21	0	153	25.5
53-54—Boston	6	260	116	33	.284	75	60	.800	32	38	20	0	126	21.0
54-55—Boston	7	299	139	53	.381	48	46	.958	43	65	26	0	152	21.7
55-56—Boston	3	124	56	28	.500	25	23	.920	24	26	4	0	79	26.3
56-57—Boston	10	440	207	67	.324	91	68	.747	61	93	27	0	202	20.2
57-58—Boston	11	457	196	67	.342	75	64	.853	71	82	20	0	198	18.0
58-59—Boston	11	460	221	72	.326	94	70	.745	76	119	28	0	214	19.5
59-60—Boston	13	468	262	80	.305	51	39	.765	48	116	27	0	199	15.3
60-61—Boston	10	337	147	50	.340	88	67	.761	43	91	33	1	167	16.7
61-62—Boston	14	474	241	86	.357	76	52	.684	64	123	43	0	224	16.0
62-63—Boston	13	413	204	72	.353	47	39	.830	32	116	44	2	183	14.1
Totals	109	3940	2116	689	.326	799	640	.801	546	937	314	4	2018	18.5

ALL-STAR GAME RECORD

Sea.—Team	Min.	FGA.	FGM.	Pct.	FTA.	FTM.	Pct.	Reb.	Ast.	PF.	Disq.	Pts.
1951—Boston	....	12	2	.167	5	4	.800	9	8	3	0	8
1952—Boston	33	14	4	.286	2	1	.500	4	13	3	0	9
1953—Boston	36	11	4	.364	7	7	1.000	5	3	1	0	15
1954—Boston	34	15	6	.400	8	8	1.000	11	4	1	0	20
1955—Boston	35	14	7	.500	7	6	.857	9	5	1	0	20
1956—Boston	24	8	2	.250	4	3	.750	7	2	6	1	7
1957—Boston	28	14	4	.286	2	2	1.000	5	7	0	0	10
1958—Boston	31	20	8	.400	6	4	.667	5	10	0	0	20
1959—Boston	32	8	4	.500	6	5	.833	5	4	0	0	13
1960—Boston	26	7	1	.143	0	0	.000	5	8	2	0	2
1961—Boston	33	11	2	.182	0	0	.000	3	8	6	1	4
1962—Boston	31	13	4	.308	4	3	.750	6	8	2	0	11
1963—Boston	25	11	4	.364	0	0	.000	4	6	2	0	8
Totals	368	158	52	.329	51	43	.843	78	86	27	2	147

Bob Cousy is the only player named to the all-NBA team for ten successive seasons (twice named to the second five).

He is also the only player to have participated in the 13 All-Star games.

The information on this and next page is from the Official 1963-64 NBA Guide.

KEY TO DIAGRAMS

path of player	——————⟶
path of ball	- - - - - ⟶
dribble	⟿
pick or screen	↙︎——

CELTICS

6—Bill Russell
14—Bob Cousy
15—Tom Heinshon
16—Tom Sanders
17—John Havlicek
18—Jim Luscutoff
23—Frank Ramsey
24—Sam Jones
25—K. C. Jones